Finding Our Way

Previous books by Margaret J. Wheatley

Turning to One Another
A Simpler Way (with Myron Kellner-Rogers)
Leadership and the New Science

Finding Our Way
Leadership for an Uncertain Time

Margaret J. Wheatley

BERRETT-KOEHLER PUBLISHERS, INC.
San Francisco

Berrett-Koehler Publishers, Inc.
235 Montgomery Street, Suite 650
San Francisco, CA 94104-2916
Tel: (415) 288-0260   Fax: (415) 362-2512   www.bkconnection.com

Ordering Information
Quantity sales. Special discounts are available on quantity purchases by corporations, associations, and others. For details, contact the "Special Sales Department" at the Berrett-Koehler address above.
Individual sales. Berrett-Koehler publications are available through most bookstores. They can also be ordered directly from Berrett-Koehler: Tel: (800) 929-2929; Fax: (802) 864-7626; www.bkconnection.com
Orders for college textbook/course adoption use. Please contact Berrett-Koehler: Tel: (800) 929-2929; Fax: (802) 864-7626.
Orders by U.S. trade bookstores and wholesalers. Please contact Publishers Group West, 1700 Fourth Street, Berkeley, CA 94710. Tel: (510) 528-1444; Fax (510) 528-3444.

Design: Canace Pulfer—A/3 Design
Production Management: Michael Bass Associates

Berrett-Koehler and the BK logo are registered trademarks of Berrett-Koehler Publishers, Inc.

Printed in the United States of America

Berrett-Koehler books are printed on long-lasting acid-free paper. When it is available, we choose paper that has been manufactured by environmentally responsible processes. These may include using trees grown in sustainable forests, incorporating recycled paper, minimizing chlorine in bleaching, or recycling the energy produced at the paper mill.

Library of Congress Cataloging-in-Publication Data

Wheatley, Margaret J.
    Finding our way: leadership for an uncertain time / by Margaret J. Wheatley.
        p.   cm.
    Includes bibliographical references.
    ISBN 978-1-57675-317-0
    1. Leadership. 2. Organizational change. 3. Social values. 4. Attitude change.
5. Cooperativeness. 6. Quality of life. I. Title: Leadership for an uncertain time. II. Title.

HD57.7.W456 2004
658.4′092—dc22

                                                                                    2004057359

First Edition
10 09 08 07 06 05   10 9 8 7 6 5 4 3 2

When the forms of an old culture are dying,
the new culture is created by a few people who are not afraid
to be insecure.

Rudolf Bahro

May this book serve all us insecure ones
May we give birth to a new culture of hope

It is not revolutions and upheavals
That clear the road to new and better days,
But revelations, lavishness and torments
Of someone's soul, inspired and ablaze.

Boris Pasternak, "After the Storm," 1958

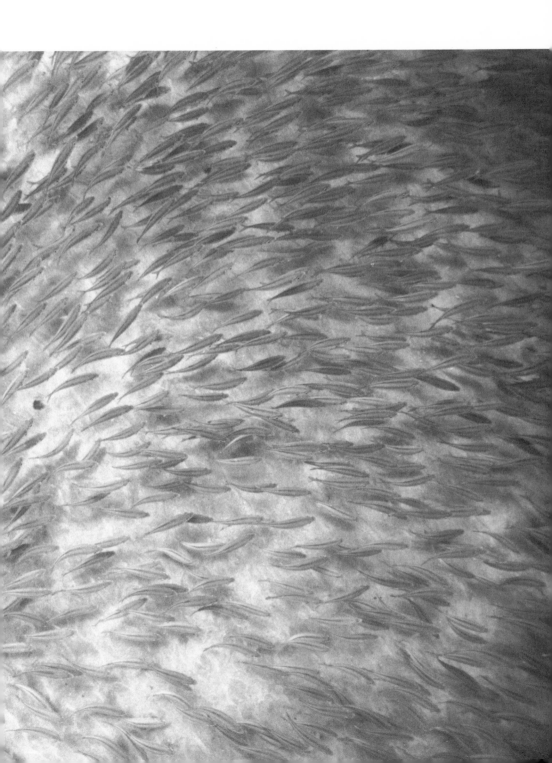

Contents

Opening

There is a simpler way to organize human endeavor. I have declared this for many years and seen it to be true in many places. This simpler way feels new, yet it is the most ancient story there is. It is the ancient story demonstrated to us daily by life, not the life we see on the news with its unending stories of human grief and horror, but what we feel when we're in nature, when we experience a sense of life's deep harmony, beauty, and power. It is the story of how we feel when we see people helping each other, when we feel creative, when we know we're making a difference, when life feels purposeful.

For many years, I've written and spoken about this ancient new story, and how we might apply it in organizations and communities around the world. I've learned that as we understand how living systems operate, we develop the skills we need: we become resilient, adaptive, aware, and creative. We enjoy working together. And life's processes work everywhere, no matter the culture, group, or person, because these are basic dynamics shared by all living beings.

As we work with life, we also rediscover another gift, the great potential of the human spirit. I've worked in many places in the world of extreme material poverty. But that challenge fades in comparison to those of us who have forgotten how resilient and vast the human spirit is. Mother Teresa once said that the greatest poverty she saw was in the West because we suffer from spiritual poverty.

Western cultural views of how best to organize and lead (the majority paradigm in use in the world) are contrary to what life teaches. Western practices attempt to dominate life; we want life to comply with human needs rather than working as partners. This disregard for life's dynamics is alarmingly evident in today's organizations. Leaders use control and imposition rather than self-organizing processes. They react to uncertainty and chaos by tightening already feeble controls, rather than engaging our best capacities in the dance. Leaders use primitive emotions of fear, scarcity, and self-interest to get people to do their work, rather than the more noble human traits of cooperation, caring, and generosity. This has led us to this difficult time, when nothing seems to work as we want it to, when too many of us feel frustrated, disengaged, and anxious.

The Era of Many Messes

I find it important, periodically, to ask people to step back and try to see the big picture. This is difficult to do when we're stressed by so many pressures at work and at home. But when we shift to fifty thousand feet, it's easier to see that our impotence is not a result of personal failings. Instead, failing to achieve good results is a consequence of living in this time when we've reached the end of a paradigm. Many of our fundamental beliefs and practices no longer serve us or the greater world. Worse than that, too many are causing harm and distancing us from the very skills, knowledge, and wisdom that would help.

This is the era of many messes. Some of these we've created (although not intentionally,) because we act on assumptions that can never engender healthy, sustainable societies and organizations. We act as if humans are motivated by selfishness, greed, and fear. That we exist as individuals, free of the obligation of interdependence. That hierarchy and bureaucracy are the best forms of organizing. That efficiency is the premier measure of value. That people work best under controls and regulations. That diversity is a problem. That unrestrained growth is good. That a healthy economy leads naturally to a healthy society.

That poor people have different motivations than other people. That only a few people are creative. That only a few people care about their freedom.

These beliefs are false. They've created the intractable problems that we now encounter everywhere. If you look globally, it's hard to find examples in any country or any major sector—health, education, religion, governance, development—of successfully solving dilemmas. Attempts to resolve them lead only to more problems, unintended consequences, and angry constituents. While millions of people work earnestly to find solutions, and billions of dollars are poured into these efforts, we can't expect success as long as we stay wedded to our old approaches.

We live in a time that proves Einstein right: "No problem can be solved from the same level of thinking that created it."

A Tale of Two Stories

This book contains many different essays, each of which was first published in a journal, magazine, or book. They represent ten years of work, of how I took the ideas in my books and applied them in practice in many different situations. However, this is not a collection of articles. I updated, revised, or substantially added to the original content of each one. In this way, everything written here represents my current views on the subjects I write about.

This book tells two stories, each meant to serve as a guide for finding our way to a more hopeful future. The first story describes and applies the new paradigm of living systems. It tells how all living systems—which includes people—self-organize, change, create, learn, and adapt. I tell this story in great detail and offer many different applications.

I hope these essays provide answers to many of the fundamental questions of leadership: How do leaders shift from control to order? What motivates people? How does change happen? How do we evoke people's innate creativity? What are useful measurement systems? How do we solve complex problems? How do we create healthy communities? How do we lead when change is out of our control? How do we maintain our integrity and peace as leaders?

Leaders and people have struggled with these questions for many years. In my experience, when we shift the paradigm, we find answers, real answers.

The second story is of a different kind. In each section, the essays appear in chronological order. I did this so you would notice the evolution of these ideas—how my topics have shifted, my emphasis has changed, and my writing has taken on a different voice. These changes illustrate how the first story fared and evolved as I took these ideas out into a world that was changing rapidly, but not in the right direction. I'm sad to report that in the past few years, ever since uncertainty became our insistent twenty-first-century companion, leadership strategies have taken *a great leap backward* to the familiar territory of command and control. Some of this was to be expected, because humans usually default to the known when confronted with the unknown. Some of it surprised me, because I thought we knew better. I thought we had learned something from all the experiments about innovation, quality, learning organizations, and human motivation. How is it that we failed to learn that whenever we try to impose control on people and situations, we only serve to make them more uncontrollable?

Whatever might explain this desperate retrenchment, for me it has made telling the new story even more important. Today, we need many more of us storytellers. The need is urgent, because people are forgetting there is any alternative to the deadening leadership that daily increases in vehemence. It's truly a dark time because people are losing faith in themselves and each other and forgetting how wonderful humans can be, how much hope we feel when we work well together on things we care about.

Because more storytellers are needed, there are essays in this book that speak to you directly. I ask you to look at how these times are affecting you personally. Do you work in ways that support interconnectedness rather than separateness? Are you taking time to think? How well do you listen to those you disagree with? What's happening with your children? Do you speak up for what you believe in?

The last part of this book is very personal. I've shared the perspectives and feelings that have arisen in me as I've been out in this troubled world. I write about my children, my country, and how I no longer seek hope, only right action. I also describe the experience of living and working in the endless spiral of paradox, especially the paradox of feeling so blessed in the peace and abundance of my life, while more and more people on this beautiful planet must confront life's horrors.

My hope is that you will feel strengthened from reading this book. I hope that your clarity grows bright and undeniable, that you have greater confidence to tell the story that is true in your experience, that you act with courage, and that you know you are in company with millions of people around the world working to bring to life this ancient new story.

The New Story in an Ancient Culture

This book came into form in a place that illuminates what it feels like to live in harmony with life and with each other, Thera Island in the Greek Aegean, near Crete. I didn't go to Thera (also named Santorini) to learn this—I innocently arrived on the island and was surprised to discover it. All I knew beforehand was that the island had been destroyed by a violent volcanic eruption around 1500 B.C.E. That eruption may have begun the end of Minoan civilization on nearby Crete, and might have destroyed Atlantis, according to the accounts of Plato.

But I was not prepared for the intense and joyful encounter I had with Theran culture when I walked into a museum shop that displayed the vivid wall murals that had adorned their buildings' interiors. I was surrounded by imagery that reflected deep harmony with life. Dolphins danced with ships, birds filled the air, and every scene was filled with flowers and animals. It felt as if I was looking at the Peaceable Kingdom where all creatures shared easily in life's pleasures. I recalled that Minoan culture was deeply feminine, led by women priests. I picked up a replica of their pottery and loved the round feminine shape of a jug where swallows flew in graceful arcs across the surface.

I felt such deep kinship with these artists and their joyous images that I needed to learn more. Who were these people who could stir my tired soul and awaken such keen curiosity to know more about their life? Here's what I learned.

Theran culture was its own unique expression of Minoan culture, a world that never fragmented nature from humans from art. Humans were not separate from the natural order. They didn't attempt to manipulate it or to observe it from a distance. I found this difficult to comprehend, coming from a culture so fixated on separation and control, where art is something different than life, where humans stand outside life and seek to control it.

Minoans expected order to triumph over chaos because they lived close to life and knew life's cyclical nature. Cycles kept them from focusing on isolated events or from thinking that life was always progressing. (These beliefs still can be found today in indigenous cultures or their traditions.) In the eternal, recurring cycles of life, incidents and dramas were of no consequence. Humans participated in a grand circular flow of life. People lived these cycles not as humans making history, but as humans living life. Nothing happened outside or independent of the living world. People didn't visit "nature" as we do now. It was all one life.

Minoans knew life to be abundant. Their paintings express joyful awareness that the earth gives great gifts of fertility and blesses us with its beautiful diversity of animals, flowers, and plants. Every painting celebrates this rich, gorgeous bounty.

All of this ended with the volcanic eruption. An ironic end to a culture that loved life, but also a firm teacher to those of us who hope to cling to what we have. Nearly a thousand years later, Greek civilization reached its zenith in Athens and set the course of Western mind that we're still dealing with today. The Greeks fell in love with themselves, with the human form, with history, with heroes. In their love of human potential, they set us on a path where we forgot that humans exist within a greater cosmos. And today, it's hard to remember what it feels like to be a beloved partner with life.

As I sat on the rim of the caldera that ended Theran life, living the good tourist life, I discovered a civilization that embodied what I know. What the Therans knew, I know, that it is possible to live and work together in ways that bring out our creativity, that inspire us to do good work, that bring more harmony and pleasure to our relationships. And I know that we get into desperate trouble, as the Greek experience teaches, when we make ourselves the only focus, when we revere heroic leaders, when we treat life as something distant from us that we ignore and occasionally visit.

The certainty of cycles, the triumph of order over chaos, the diversity born from life's creativity, the innate artistry of each of us, the enduring beauty of the human spirit—these are what I write about. From Minoan times till now, the story hasn't changed. But it is important that we reclaim it and retell it before we are swept away by eruptions of our own making.

Margaret J. Wheatley
October, 2004

Ancient Thera, Modern Teacher

The wind working its
    way through ancient
        cracks and ill-fitting doors pestered
           me all night.

Now it is morning and
    nothing has settled down the
        wind refuses to clear a space
           for contemplation. This is stormy

country, lost to fire and sea, buried by meters and
    meters of hard pumice rain and heavy boulders,
        the volcano falling into its

fiery heart and sea blazing in to fill the steaming
    crater that once was island.
        Gorgeous culture ended here.

        Island home to painters who knew
           no restraint who took ceremonial rooms and

made them come alive with color and
    form bound by no convention
        strong joyful brush strokes bringing

life to barren walls on barren
land their homes painted still today
reminding us of times when

dolphins danced with fleets and
swallows swept the wild sea air
with song. Even now when

it all collapsed and 2500 years of
grief and dust had to be gently cleansed
to see their life even now Minoan joy

is here and even now their happy
life lifts my human heart above
my own ruined time and

reminds me that life can be
good even when lived in the shadow of
what must destroy it.

They knew what was coming.

Many times tremors and ash
warned them to take their
treasures and flee yet they
returned to clean and

rebuild and recreate the life they loved

and then the volcano would

have no more of them and

Earth erupted with the violence

only found deep inside

creation. All fire the

blast blew black obsidian boulders like dust,

mythic energy reminding humans

how tenderly to walk

the earth that goes from beloved

to fire when it tolerates us

no longer.

Thera, Greece, May 2004

Organizing
There Is a Simpler Way

Each of these essays describes the new story, describing different capabilities and dynamics of all living systems, including people. This is the foundation, the theory base, for all that follows in later essays when I apply these dynamics to leadership and organizational practices.

The whole globe is shook up, so what are you going to do when things are falling apart? You're either going to become more fundamentalist and try to hold things together, or you're going to forsake the old ambitions and goals and live life as an experiment, making it up as you go along.

—Pema Chödrön

The New Story Is Ours to Tell

Willis Harman, an invaluable mentor to me and many people, changed my work with a letter he wrote me in 1994. Willis urged me to continue speaking my message but warned me not to derive it solely from science. As he did with so many, he wanted me to understand the deeper premises of modern science, which, for all the "new science" hoopla, were anything but new. He encouraged me to explore the deeper values and premises of my work that were far more important than any science.

I contemplated his letter for months. I realized that I was using the science to get the attention of those who could hear this message in no other form. (When I told Willis this, he laughed and applauded my clarity. If you're being Machiavellian, it's good to realize it.) What was "my message" from the new sciences has grown in depth and strength into a "new story." It is sourced from many traditions, not just Western science, and I offer it to any individual or group that is willing to listen. I am less focused on persuasion and more engaged in the telling of a story that gives hope and possibility to us all.

Many people hold this new story. Traditional cultures have held it for centuries, even as they've been told their ways are primitive or backward. But for us growing up in the West, many of us falter in expressing this voice because we've been told that these ideas which we feel intuitively—about leaders, organizations, and people—are crazy. It is time to change this definition of craziness. We, in fact, represent *the new sanity*—the ideas and values and practices that can create a future worth wanting.

Those who carry a new story and who risk speaking it abroad have played a crucial role in times of historic shift. Before a new era can come into form, there must be a new story. The playwright Arthur Miller noted that we know an era has ended when its basic illusions have been exhausted. I would add that these basic illusions not only are exhausted but also have become exhausting.

As they fail to produce the results we want, we just repeat them with greater desperation, plummeting ourselves into cynicism and despair as we lock into these cycles of failure.

I was introduced to the critical nature of the teller-of-new-stories role in reading the work of physicist Brian Swimme and theologian Thomas Berry. They wrote a new story of the universe, based on their belief that creating a new cosmic story is the most important work of our times. It is the new stories that will usher in a new era of human and planetary health.

Lest you believe that cosmic stories can only be told by physicists or theologians, their idea of a cosmic story is one that answers such questions as, What's going on? Where did everything come from? Why are you doing what you do?

I believe that you and I have important themes to contribute to this new cosmic story. I would like to contrast in some detail the new and the old stories. My hope is that in seeing the great polarities between these two, you will feel more strongly called to give voice to the new.

For more than three hundred years, Western culture has been developing the old story. I would characterize it as a story of dominion and control, and all-encompassing materialism. This story began with a dream that it was within humankind's province to understand the workings of the universe, and to gain complete mastery over physical matter. This dream embraced the image of the universe as a grand, clockwork machine. As with any machine, we would understand it by minute dissection, we would engineer it to do what we saw fit, and we would fix it through our engineering brilliance. This hypnotic image of powers beyond previous human imagination gradually was applied to everything we looked at: our bodies were seen as the ultimate machines; our organizations had all the parts and specifications to assure well-oiled performance; and in science, where it all began, many scientists confused metaphor with reality and believed life *was* a machine.

This dream still has immense hypnotic power over us. For every problem, we quickly leap to technical solutions, even if technology is the cause of the initial problem. Science will still save us, no matter the earthly mess we've created. In our bodies, we long to believe the promises of genetic engineering. Our greatest ills, perhaps even death, will vanish once we identify the troubling gene. We need only invest more in technology to yield unsurpassed benefits in health and longevity, and all because we are such smart engineers of the human body.

In most of our endeavors—in science, health, management, self-help—the focus is on creating better-functioning machines We replace the faulty part, reengineer the organization, install a new behavior or attitude, create a better fit, recharge our batteries. The language and thinking is mechanistic. And we give this image such hegemony over our lives because it seems our only hope for combating life's cyclical nature, our one hope of escape from life's incessant demands for creation and destruction.

When we created this story of complete dominion over matter, we also brought in control's unwelcome partner, fear. Once we are intent on controlling something, we feel afraid when we meet with resistance. Since nothing is as controllable as we hope, we soon become entangled in a cycle of exerting control, failing to control, exerting harsher control, failing again, panicking. The fear that arises from this cycle is notable in many of us. It's especially notable in our leaders. Things aren't working as they had hoped, but none of us knows any other way to proceed. The world becomes scarier as we see daily the results of our ignorance and confront our true powerlessness. It is from this place, from an acknowledgment of our ignorance and lack of power, that the call goes out for a new story.

But the old story has some further dimensions worth noticing. This story has had a particularly pernicious effect on how we think about one another, and how we approach the task of organizing any human endeavor. When we conceived of ourselves as machines, we gave up most of what is essential to being human. We created ourselves devoid of spirit, will, passion, compassion, emotions, even intelligence. Machines have none of these characteristics innately, and none of them can be built into its specifications. The imagery is so foreign to what we know and feel to be true about ourselves that it seems strange that we ever adopted this as an accurate description of being human. But we did, and we do. A colleague of mine, as he was about to work with a group of oil company engineers, was warned that they had "heads of cement." He cheerfully remarked that it didn't matter, because they all had hearts, didn't they? "Well," they replied, "we call it a pump."

The engineering image we carry of ourselves has led to organizational lives where we believe we can ignore the deep realities of human existence. We can ignore that people carry spiritual questions and quests into their work; we can ignore that people need love and acknowledgment; we can pretend that emotions are not part of our work lives; we can pretend we don't have families, or health crises, or deep worries. In essence, we take the complexity of human life and organize it away. It is not part of the story we want to believe. We want a story of simple dimensions: People can be viewed as machines and controlled to perform with the same efficiency and predictability.

It is important to recognize that people *never* behave like machines. When given directions, we insist on putting our unique spin on them. When told to follow orders, we resist in obvious or subtle ways. When told to accept someone else's solution or to institute a program created elsewhere, we deny that it has sufficient value.

As leaders, when we meet with such nonmechanical responses, we've had two options. We could criticize our own leadership skills, or we could blame our followers. If we the leader was the problem, perhaps it was due to poor communication skills; perhaps we weren't visionary enough; maybe we'd chosen the wrong sales technique. If "our people" were the problem, it was because they lacked motivation or a clear sense of responsibility, or it could be that this time we'd just been cursed with an obstinate and rebellious group. With so much blame looking for targets, we haven't taken time to stop and question our basic beliefs about each other. Are expectations of machinelike obedience and regularity even appropriate when working together?

Trying to be an effective leader in this machine story is especially exhausting. He or she is leading a group of lifeless, empty automatons who are just waiting to be filled with vision and direction and intelligence. The leader is responsible for providing everything: the organizational mission and values, the organizational structure, the plans, the supervision. The leader must also figure out, through clever use of incentives or coercives, how to pump energy into this lifeless mass. Once the pump is primed, he must then rush hither and yon to make sure that everyone is clanking along in the same direction, at the established speed, with no diversions. It is the role of the leader to provide the organizing energy for a system that is believed to have no internal capacities for self-creation, self-organization, or self-correction.

As I reflect on the awful demands placed on leaders by the old story, I wonder how anyone could survive in that job. Yet the mechanistic story has created roles for all of us that are equally deadly. It has led us to believe that we, with our unpredictable behaviors, our passions, our independence, our creativity, our consciousness—that we are the problem rather than the blessing. While the rest of nature follows obediently in the great mechanistic parade of progress, we humans show up as rebellious and untrustworthy. Our problematic natures are the very reason we need to create organizations as we do. How else could we structure such recalcitrance into vehicles of efficient production?

In this story, such key human traits as uniqueness, free will, and creativity pose enormous problems. Machines are built to do repetitive functions that require no thought and minimal adjustment. Conformity and compliance are part of the expectations of this story. Creativity is unwanted, because it is always surprising and therefore uncontrollable. If we tolerate creative expressions, we find ourselves with unmanageable levels of diversity. A machine world is willing to sacrifice exploration for prediction. Guaranteed levels of performance are preferable to surprising breakthroughs. In our machine-organizations, we try to extinguish individuality in order to reach our goal of compliance. We trade uniqueness for control, and barter our humanness for petty performance measures.

It is one of the great ironies of our age that we created organizations to constrain our problematic human natures, and now the only thing that can save these organizations is a full appreciation of the expansive capacities of us humans.

So it is time for the new story. Our old one, with its alienating myths, is eating away at us from the inside, rotting from its core. Fewer of us tell it with conviction. Many more of us are beginning to understand that our experience and our beliefs tell a story that celebrates life rather than denying it. We can see these in the pronounced increase in conversations and writings about destiny, purpose, soul, spirit, love, legacy, courage, integrity, meaning. The new story is being born in these conversations. We are learning to give voice to a different and fuller sense of who we really are.

I would like to characterize the new story as a tale of life. Setting aside our machine glasses, we can observe a world that exhibits life's ebullient creativity and life's great need for other life. We observe a world where creative self-expression and embracing systems of relationships are the organizing energies, where there is no such thing as an independent individual, and no need for a leader to take on as much responsibility for us as we've demanded in the past.

As I develop some of the major themes of this new story of life, I will be drawing first on the work of modern science. However, science is only the most recent contributor to a story that is very ancient. We find this story in primal wisdom traditions, in indigenous tribes, in most spiritual thought, and in poets old and new. It is a story that has never been forgotten by any of us, and that has been held for us continually by many peoples and cultures. Yet for those of us emerging from our exhaustion with the old mechanistic tale, it feels new. And it certainly opens us to new discoveries about who we are as people, as organizations, and as leaders.

For me, one of the most wonderful contrasts of the old and new stories is described in a passage in Kevin Kelly's book *Out of Control*. As he reached for language to describe life, he moved into sheer exuberance. (I always pay attention when a scientist uses poetic language—I know that something has touched him or her at a level of awareness that I don't want to ignore.) Kelly was trying to describe the ceaseless creativity that characterizes life. He said that life gives to itself this great freedom, the freedom to become. Then he asked, "Becoming what?" and went on to answer:

> Becoming becoming. Life is on its way to further complications, further deepness and mystery, further processes of becoming and change. Life is circles of becoming, an autocatalytic set, inflaming itself with its own sparks, breeding upon itself more life and more wildness and more "becomingness." Life has no conditions, no moments that are not instantly becoming something more than life itself. (Kelly, 110)

Kelly's passionate descriptions of processes that inflame, breed more life and wildness, create more deepness and mystery, stand in stark contrast to the expectations we have held for one another. I like to contemplate Kelly's description of life with the lives we describe when we design an organizational chart. The contrast between the two is both funny and sobering. Could we even begin to tolerate such levels of passion and creativity in our organizations? But can we survive without them?

In the 1960s, the great American poet A. R. Ammons told the same story in different and precise language:

Don't establish the

boundaries

first

the squares, triangles,

boxes

of preconceived

possibility,

and then

pour

life into them, trimming

off left-over edges,

ending potential:

let centers

proliferate

from

    self-justifying motions!

In both science and poetry, we are remembering a story about life that has creativity and connectedness as its essential themes. As we use this new story to look into our organizational lives, it offers us images of organizations and leaders that are both startling and enticing. It offers us ways of being together where our diversity—our uniqueness—is essential and important. It offers us an arena big enough to embrace the full expression of our infinitely creative human natures.

And for the first time in a long time, it offers us the recognition that we humans are, in the words of physicist Ilya Prigogine, "the most striking realization of the laws of nature." We can use ourselves and what we know about ourselves to understand the universe. By observing with new eyes the processes of creation in us, we can understand the forces that create galaxies, move continents, and give birth to stars. No longer intent on describing ourselves as the machines we thought the universe to be, we are encouraged now to describe the universe through the life we know we are.

As we look at life through the lens of human nature and human desire, we are presented with some wonderful realizations. Our own desire for autonomy and creativity is reflected in all life. Life appears as boundlessly creative, search-ing for new possibilities and new capacities wherever it can. Observing the diversity of life forms has become a humbling experience for many biologists. At this point, no one knows how many different species there are or where the next forms of life will appear, except that now we even expect them to appear elsewhere in our solar system.

Life is born from this unquenchable need to be. One of the most interesting definitions of life in modern biology is that something is considered alive if it has the capacity to create itself. The term for this is *autopoiesis*—self-creation. Life begins from the desire to create something original, to bring a new being into form.

The incredible diversity of life bears witness to a level of creativity that has little to do with the survival struggles that have been used to explain everything.

Newness appears not for simple utilitarian purposes, but just because it is possible to be inventive. Life gives to itself the freedom to become, as Kevin Kelly notes, because life is about discovering new possibilities, new forms of expression. Two biologists, Francisco Varela and Humberto Maturana, observe that life responds not to "survival of the fittest" but to the greater space of experimentation of "survival of the fit." Many designs, many adaptations are possible, and organisms enjoy far more freedom to experiment than we humans, with our insane demand to "Get it right the first time."

The freedom to experiment, to tinker oneself into a form of being that can live and reproduce, leads to diversity that has no bounds. In my own telling of a new cosmic story, I would sing that newness is a primary value embraced by all life, one that encourages life to new discoveries. The need and ability to create one's self is a force we see quite clearly in human experience but that we have greatly misunderstood in our organizations.

The second great force I would add to this new story is that life needs to link with other life, to form systems of relationships where all individuals are better supported by the system they have created. It is impossible to look into the natural world and find a separated individual. As an African proverb states: "Alone, I have seen many marvelous things, none of which were true." Biologist Lynn Margulis expresses a similar realization when she comments that independence is a political concept, not a biological concept. Everywhere life displays itself as complex, tangled, messy webs of relationships. From these relationships, life creates systems that offer greater stability and support than life lived alone. Organisms shape themselves in response to their neighbors and their environments. All respond to one another, coevolving and cocreating the complex systems of organization that we see in nature. Life is systems seeking. It seeks organization. Organization is a naturally occurring phenomenon. Self-organization is a powerful force that creates the systems we observe and testifies to a world that knows how to organize from the inside out.

Self-organizing systems have the capacity to create for themselves the aspects of organization that we thought leaders had to provide. Self-organizing systems create structures and pathways, networks of communication, values and meaning, behaviors and norms. In essence, they do for themselves most of what we believed we had to do for them. Rather than thinking of organization as an imposed structure, plan, design, or role, it is clear that in life, organization arises from the interactions and needs of individuals who have decided to come together.

The clash of the old and new stories can be seen everywhere. It is painfully visible in organizations that were created to birth the new story, including many nonprofits, churches, and public benefit organizations. People form these organizations in response to the call of the new story; they join together because they know that they can't birth this dream alone. An organization is required in order to move it forward. The human desires that lead them to organize—to find more meaning in life, to bring more good into the world, to serve others—come from the new story.

Yet as soon as they embark on the task of creating an organization, old ideas and habits arise. These organizations impose structures and roles, develop elaborate plans, use command and control leadership. Over time, the organization that was created in response to the new story becomes a rigid structure exemplifying, yet again, the old story. People come to resent the organization they created, because now it is a major impediment to their creativity, to their hope, to their dreams.

The new story holds out different images of organization—it teaches us that humans, when joined together, are capable of giving birth to the form of the organization, to the plans, to the values, to the vision. All of life is self-organizing, and so are we. But the new story also details a process for organizing that stands in shocking contrast to the images of well-planned, well-orchestrated, well-supervised organizing. I can summarize the organizing processes of life quite simply: Life seeks organization, but it uses messes to get there. Organization is a process, not a structure.

Simultaneously, the process of organizing involves developing relationships from a shared sense of purpose, exchanging and creating information, learning constantly, paying attention to the results of our efforts, coadapting, coevolving, developing wisdom as we learn, staying clear about our purpose, being alert to changes from all directions. Living systems give form to their organization and evolve those forms into new ones, because of exquisite capacities to create meaning together, to communicate, and to notice what's going on in the moment. These are the capacities that give any organization its true aliveness, that support self-organization.

In the new story, we discover a world where life gives birth to itself using two powerful forces: the need to be free to create one's self and the need to reach out for relationships with others. These forces never disappear from life. Even if we deny them, we can't ever extinguish them. They are always active, even in the most repressive human organizations. Life can never stop asserting its need to create itself, and life never stops searching for connections.

We fail to acknowledge these unstoppable forces of life whenever we, as leaders, try to direct and control those in our organization. Life always pushes back against our demands. But instead of learning about life, we tend to see their "difficult" behaviors as justification for a more controlling style of leadership. Many of the failures and discontents in today's organizations can be understood as the result of this denial of life's forces and how life pushes back against a story that excludes it.

To see these competing forces, think about how many times you have engaged in conversations about "resistance to change." I have participated in far too many of these, and in the old days, when I still thought that it was me who was "managing" change, my colleagues and I always were thoughtful enough to plan a campaign to overcome this resistance. Contrast this view of human resistance to change with Kelly's images of life as "further processes of becoming and change . . . circles of becoming, inflaming itself with its own sparks, breeding upon itself more life and more wildness." Who's telling the right story? Do we, as a species, dig in our heels while the rest of life is engaged in this awesome dance of creation? Are we the only problem, whereas the rest of life participates in something wild and wonderful?

The old story asserts that resistance to change is a fact of life. Bound by a world view that seeks stability and control, change is always undesirable. But the new story explains resistance not as a fact of life, but as evidence of an act *against* life. Life is in motion, constantly creating, exploring, discovering. Nothing alive, including us, resists these great creative motions. But all of life resists control. All of life reacts to any process that inhibits its freedom to create itself.

In organizations of the old story, plans and designs are constantly being imposed. People are told what to do all the time. As a final insult, leaders go outside the organization to look for answers, returning with programs and methods invented elsewhere. Those in the organization only see these prepackaged solutions as insults. Their creativity has been dismissed, their opportunity to invent something new for the organization has been denied. When we deny life's need to create, life pushes back. We label it resistance and invent strategies to overcome it. But we would do far better if we changed the story and learned how to invoke the resident creativity of those in our organization. We need to work with these insistent creative forces or they will be provoked to work against us.

And most organizations deny the systems-seeking, self-organizing forces that are always present, the forces that, in fact, are responsible for uncharted levels of contribution and innovation. These fail to get reported because they occur outside "the boxes of preconceived possibility." There is no better indicator of the daily but unrecognized contributions made by people than when a municipal union, prohibited from going on strike, decides to "work to rule." They work *only* according to the rule book. They *only* follow policies and job descriptions. The great irony is that even though rules and policies are designed to create productive work, as soon as they are the only instructions, cities cease running, effective civil functioning stops. What work-to-rule demonstrates is that no organization functions on the *planned* contributions of its members. Every organization relies on its employees going beyond the rules and roles, figuring out what needs to be done, solving unexpected problems as they appear.

We also deny these system-seeking forces when we narrow people to self-serving work, when we pit colleagues against one another to improve performance, when we believe people are most strongly motivated by promises of personal gain. If we deny people's great need for relationships, for systems of support, for work that connects to a larger purpose, they push back. They may respond first by embracing competition but then lose interest in the incentives. Performance falls back to precontest levels. In organizations driven by greed, people push back by distrusting and despising their leaders. In organizations that try to substitute monetary rewards for a true purpose, people respond with apathy and disaffection.

It is possible to look at the negative and troubling behaviors in organizations today as the clash between the forces of life and the forces of domination, between the new story and the old. Once we realize that we cannot ever extinguish these creative forces, that it is impossible to deny the life that lives in our organizations, we can begin to search for new ways of being together.

In many different places, the new story is emerging. It is, in its essence, a story about the human spirit. This realization is surfacing in many different disciplines and people. For those who have focused on organizations, I find it delightful to note that two great management thinkers, Edward Deming, the great voice for quality in organizations, and Robert Greenleaf, the prophet of servant leadership, both focused on the human spirit in their final writings. Deming concluded his long years of work by stating simply that quality was about the human spirit. As we grew to understand that spirit, we would create organizations of quality. Greenleaf understood that we stood as servants to the human spirit, that it was our responsibility to nurture that spirit. Following different paths, they arrived at the same centering place. We can create the lives and organizations we desire only by understanding the enlivening spirit in us that always is seeking to express itself.

Leaders who live in the new story help us understand ourselves differently by the way they lead. They trust our humanness; they welcome the surprises we bring to them; they are curious about our differences; they delight in our inventiveness; they nurture us; they connect us. They trust that we can create wisely and well, that we seek the best interests of our organization and our community, that we want to bring more good into the world.

We who hold this story feel both its beauty and its promise. What might we create if we lived our lives closer to the human spirit? What might our organizations accomplish if they trusted and called on that spirit? I want us to be telling this story in health care organizations, on campuses, in schools, in governments, in religious denominations, in corporations. I want traditional business/economic logic to stop being the only story; I want business/economic imperatives to stop moving us away from the deeper realities we know. Even in the for-profit sector where it still dominates, the old story has not created organizations that are sustainable over time or welcoming of the human spirit.

Why would we let such thinking move unchallenged into other types of organizations or other cultures?

When it is time for a new story to emerge, holding onto the past only intensifies our dilemma. We experience our ineffectiveness daily, and we descend into a profound sense of lost. What we ask of the tellers of the new story is their voice and their courage. We do not need them to create a massive training program, a global approach, a dramatic style. We only need them to speak to us when we are with them. We need them to break their silence and share their ideas of the world as they have come to know it.

If you carry this story within you, it is time to tell it, wherever you are, to whomever you meet. Brian Swimme compares our role to that of the early Christians. They had nothing but "a profound revelatory experience. They did nothing—nothing but wander about telling a new story." As with these early believers, Brian encourages us to become wanderers, telling our new story. Through our simple wanderings, we will "ignite the transformation of humanity." And he leaves us with a promise:

> What will happen when the storytellers emerge? What will happen when "the primal mind" sings of our common origin, our stupendous journey, our immense good fortune? We will become Earthlings. We will have evoked out of the depths of the human psyche those qualities enabling our transformation from disease to health. They will sing our epic of being, and stirring up from our roots will be a vast awe, an enduring gratitude, the astonishment of communion experiences, and the realization of cosmic adventure.

What a wonderful promise. I invite you into the telling.

The Irresistible Future of Organizing

with Myron Rogers

Why do so many people in organizations feel discouraged and fearful about the future? Why does despair only increase as the fads fly by, shorter in duration, more costly in each attempt to improve? Why have the best efforts to create significant and enduring organizational change resulted in so many failures? We, and our organizations, exist in a world of constant evolutionary activity. Why is change so unnatural in human organizations?

The accumulating failures at organizational change can be traced to a fundamental but mistaken assumption that organizations are machines. Organizations-as-machines is a seventeenth-century notion, from a time when philosophers began to describe the universe as a great clock. Our modern belief in prediction and control originated in these clockwork images. Cause and effect were simple relationships. Everything could be known. Organizations and people could be engineered into efficient solutions. Three hundred years later, we still search for "tools and techniques" and "change levers"; we attempt to "drive" change through our organizations; we want to "build" solutions and "reengineer" for peak efficiencies.

But why would we want an organization to behave like a machine? Machines have no intelligence; they follow the instructions given to them. They only work in the specific conditions predicted by their engineers. Changes in their environment wreak havoc because they have no capacity to adapt.

These days, a different ideal for organizations is surfacing. We want organizations to be adaptive, flexible, self-renewing, resilient, learning, intelligent—attributes found only in living systems. The tension of our times is that we want our organizations to behave as living systems, but we only know how to treat them as machines.

It is time to change the way we think about organizations. Organizations are living systems. All living systems have the capacity to *self-organize*, to sustain themselves and move toward greater complexity and order as needed. They can respond intelligently to the need for change. They organize (and then reorganize) themselves into adaptive patterns and structures without any externally imposed plan or direction.

Self-organizing systems have what all leaders crave: the capacity to respond continuously to change. In these systems, change is the organizing force, not a problematic intrusion. Structures and solutions are temporary. Resources and people come together to create new initiatives, to respond to new regulations, to shift the organization's processes. Leaders emerge from the needs of the moment. There are far fewer levels of management. Experimentation is the norm. Local solutions predominate but are kept local, not elevated to models for the whole organization. Involvement and participation constantly deepen. These organizations are experts at the process of change. They understand their organization as a process of continuous organizing.

Self-organization offers hope for a simpler and more effective way to accomplish work. It challenges the most fundamental assumptions about how organization happens and the role of leaders. But it is not a new phenomenon. We have lived our entire lives in a self-organizing world. We watch self-organization on TV in the first hours after any disaster. People and resources organize without planning into coordinated, purposeful activity. Leaders emerge and recede based on who is available and who has information. Everything happens quickly and a little miraculously. These self-organized efforts create effective responses long before official relief agencies can even make it to the scene.

In the history of organizational theory, people have commented on self-organization for many years. Years ago, we called it the "informal organization." This was a description of what people did in order to accomplish their work.

Often people ignored the formal structures, finding them ineffective and unresponsive. They reached out for the resources and relationships they needed; they followed leaders of their own choosing, those they knew they could rely on.

A more recent description of self-organization is found in "communities of practice." These communities are webs of connections woven by people to get their work done. For example, technical people reach out, both within and beyond their company, to find answers to technical questions. Over time, they develop new knowledge that benefits the company and also find supportive colleagues.

The World Wide Web is the most potent and visible example of a self-organizing network forming around interests, the availability of information, and unbounded access to one another. It will be interesting to observe the Web's future now that control issues, both content and spam, have become paramount concerns.

While there are many other examples of self-organization occurring in our midst, including well-documented experiences with self-managed teams, we will simply note that self-organization is not a new phenomenon. It has been difficult to observe only because we weren't interested in observing it. But as we describe organizations as living systems rather than as machines, self-organization becomes a primary concept, easily visible.

Order in Complex Systems

In the natural sciences, the search to understand self-organization derives from a very large question. How does life create greater order over time? Order is the unique ability of living systems to organize, reorganize, and grow more complex. But theoretical biologist Stuart Kauffman has demonstrated that the inevitable desire to organize is evident even in a nonliving system of light bulbs.

Kauffman constructed a network of two hundred light bulbs, connecting one bulb to the behavior of only two others (using Boolean logic). For example, light bulb 23 could be instructed to go on if bulb 46 went on and to go off if bulb 67 went on. The assigned connections were always random and limited to only two. Once the network was switched on, different configurations of on/off bulbs would illuminate. The number of possible on/off configurations is 10^{30}, a number of inconceivable possibilities. Given these numbers, we would expect chaos to rule. But it doesn't. The system settles instantly (on about the fourteenth iteration) into a pattern of on/off bulbs that it then continues to repeat.

A few simple connections are sufficient to generate orderly patterns. Complex behavior originates from simple rules of connection. Order is not predesigned or engineered from the outside. The system organizes itself. We live in a universe, states Kauffman, where we get "order for free."

Emergence: The Surprise of Complexity

Social insects, bird flocks, schools of fish, human traffic jams, all exhibit well-synchronized, highly ordered behaviors. Yet these sophisticated movements are not directed by any leader. Instead, a few rules focused at the local level lead to coordinated responses. Computer simulations that mimic flocking, swarming, or schooling behaviors program in only two or three rules for individuals to follow. There is never a rule about a leader or direction. The rules focus only on an individual's behavior in relation to that of its neighbors. Synchronized behavior emerges without orchestrated planning. (Recent commentators on the history of science note that scientists consistently avoided the conclusion that there was no leader. The belief in the need for planning and authority runs deep in Western thought.)

A startling example of complex and coordinated behavior emerging without leaders or plans is found in tower-building termites. In Africa and Australia, these termites build intricate, tall towers; these are the largest structures on earth proportionate to the size of their builders. They are engineering marvels, filled with intricate chambers, tunnels, arches, and air-conditioning and humidifying capabilities. Termites accomplish this feat by following a bizarre job description. They wander at will, bump up against one another, and react. They observe what others are doing and coordinate their own activities with that information. Without blueprints or engineers, their arches meet in the middle.

Whether it be light bulbs, birds, termites, or humans, the conditions that create organization are the same. Individuals are similarly focused. Members develop connections with one another. Each determines its behavior based on information about what its neighbors are doing and what the collective purpose is. From such simple conditions, working communities emerge, self-organizing from local connections into global patterns and processes. Nothing is pre-planned; patterns of behavior emerge that could not be predicted from observing individuals.

There is much to startle us in these scientific visions of how life organizes itself. Can human organizations be more intentionally self-organizing?

Three Conditions of Self-organizing Organizations
If complex systems emerge from simple initial conditions, then human organizations similarly can be rooted in simplicity. During the past few years, our own search has focused on the simple conditions that support an organization's capacity to access its intelligence and to change as needed. We have seen evidence of these conditions in a wide variety of settings: in worldwide manufacturers, in schools, in experiments with future battle strategy in the U.S. Army.

Organizations assume different forms, but they emerge from fundamentally similar conditions. A self gets organized. A world of shared meaning develops. Networks of relationships take form. Information is noticed, interpreted, transformed. From these simple dynamics emerge widely different expressions of organization. We have identified these essentials as three primary domains: identity, information, and relationships.

Identity: The Sense-making Capacity of the Organization
How does an organization spin itself into existence? All organizing efforts begin with an intent, a belief that something more is possible now that the group is together. Organizing occurs around an identity—there is a "self" that gets organized. Once this identity is set in motion, it becomes the sense-making process of the organization. In deciding what to do, a system will refer back to its sense of self. We all interpret events and data according to who we think we are. We never simply "know" the world; we create worlds based on the meaning we invest in the information we choose to notice. Thus, everything we know is determined by who we think we are.

As we create perceptions of the world, we primarily use information that is *already in us* to make sense of something new. Biologists Humberto Maturana and Francisco Varela explain that more than 80 percent of the information we use to create visual perceptions of the world comes from information already *inside* the brain. Less than 20 percent of the information we use to create a perception is external to the brain. Information from the outside only perturbs a system; it never functions as objective instructions. Maturana and Varela describe this in an important maxim: "You can never direct a living system. You can only disturb it" (162). This explains why organizations reject reports and data that others assume to be obvious and compelling. A system will be disturbed by information based on what's going on inside the organization—how the organization understands itself at that moment. This maxim also explains why organizations are never changed by assembling a new set of plans, by implementation directives or by organizational restructurings. You can never direct a living system; you can only disturb it.

The self the organization references includes its vision, mission, and values. But there is more. An organization's identity includes current interpretations of its history, present decisions and activities, and its sense of its future. Identity is both what we want to believe is true and what our actions show to be true about ourselves.

Because identity is the sense-making capacity of the organization, every organizing effort—whether it be the start-up of a team, a community project, or a nation—needs to begin by exploring and clarifying the intention and desires of its members. Why are we doing this? What's possible now that we've agreed to try this together? How does the purpose of this effort connect to my personal sense of purpose and to the purposes of the large system?

Think for a moment of your own experiences with the start-up activities of new projects or teams. Did the group spend much time discussing the deeper and often murkier realms of purpose and commitment? Or did people just want to know what their role was so they could get out of the meeting and get on with it? Did leaders spend more time on policies and procedures to coerce people into contributing rather than try to engage their desire to contribute to a worthy purpose?

Most organizing efforts don't begin with a commitment to creating a coherent sense of identity. Yet it is this clarity that frees people to contribute in creative and diverse ways. Clear alignment around principles and purposes allows for maximum autonomy. People use their shared sense of identity to organize their unique contributions.

Organizations lose an enormous organizing advantage when they fail to create a clear and coherent identity. In a chaotic world, organizational identity needs to be the most stable aspect of the endeavor. Structures and programs come and go, but an organization with a coherent center is able to sustain itself through turbulence because of its clarity about who it is. Organizations that are coherent at their core move through the world with more confidence. Such clarity leads to expansionary behaviors; the organization expands to include those they had kept at a distance—customers, suppliers, government regulators, and many others.

Information: The Medium of the Organization
Information lies at the heart of life. Life uses information to organize itself into material form. What is information? We like Gregory Bateson's definition, "Information is a difference which makes a difference," and Stafford Beer's explanation, "Information is that which changes us." When a system assigns meaning to data, when it "in-forms" it, data then becomes information.

Complex, living systems thrive in a zone of exquisitely sensitive information processing, on a constantly changing edge between stability and chaos that has been dubbed "the edge of chaos." In this dynamic region, new information can enter, but the organization retains its identity. Contradicting most efforts to keep organizations at equilibrium, living systems seem to seek this far-from-equilibrium condition to stay alive. If a system has too much order, it atrophies and dies. Yet if it lives in chaos, it has no memory. Examples of both these behaviors abound in corporate America. Over and over, we see organizations flounder because their sophisticated information and measurement systems created a sense of internal order while failing to look at critical new information. And many businesses move into new markets and businesses chaotically, with no experience to manage them effectively.

Information that flows openly through an organization often looks chaotic. But it is the nutrient of self-organization. As one utility chief executive aptly put it: "In our organization, information has gone from being the *currency of exchange—*

we traded it for power and status—to being the *medium* of our organization. We can't live without it; everyone feeds off of it. It has to be everywhere in the organization to sustain us."

Only when information belongs to everyone can people organize rapidly and effectively around shifts in customers, competitors, or environments. People need access to information that no one could predict they would want to know. They themselves didn't know they needed it until that very moment.

To say that information belongs to everyone doesn't mean that all decisions move to the most local units. When information is available everywhere, different people see different things. Those with a more strategic focus will see opportunities that others can't discern. Those on a production line similarly will pick up on information that others ignore. There is a need for many more eyes and ears, for many more members of the organization to "in-form" the available data so that effective self-organization can occur. But it is information—unplanned, uncontrolled, abundant, superfluous—that creates the conditions for the emergence of fast, well-integrated, effective responses.

Relationships: The Pathways of Organization
Relationships are the pathways to the intelligence of the system. Through relationships, information is created and transformed, the organization's identity expands to include more stakeholders, and the enterprise becomes wiser. The more access people have to one another, the more possibilities there are. Without connections, nothing happens. Organizations held at equilibrium by well-designed organization charts die. In self-organizing systems, people need access to everyone; they need to be free to reach anywhere in the organization to accomplish work.

To respond with speed and effectiveness, people need access to the intelligence of the whole system. Who is available, what do they know, and how can they reach each other? People need opportunities to "bump up" against others in the system, making the unplanned connections that spawn new ventures or better-integrated responses.

Where members of an organization have access to one another, the system expands to include more and more of them as stakeholders. It is astonishing to see how many of the behaviors we fear in one another dissipate in the presence of good relationships. Customers engaged in finding a solution become less insistent on perfection or detailed up-front specifications. Colleagues linked by a work project become more tolerant of one another's diverse lives. A community invited into a local chemical plant learns how a failure at the plant could create devastating environmental disasters, yet becomes more trusting of plant leadership.

The Dynamics of Self-organization

The domains of identity, information, and relationships operate in a dynamic cycle so intertwined that it becomes difficult to distinguish among the three elements. New relationships connect more and more of the system, creating information that affects the organization's identity. Similarly, as information circulates freely, it creates new business and propels people into new relationships. As the organization responds to new information and new relationships, its identity becomes clearer at the same time that it changes.

Earlier we stated that self-organization is not new in our experience of organizations; it just takes different eyes to see it. Self-organization has been going on all the time, but our attention has been diverted to perfecting the controls and mechanisms that we thought were making work happen. It is our belief that most people, whatever their organization, are using information, relationships, and identity to get work done. They work with whatever information is available, but it is usually insufficient and of poor quality. If they need more, they create misinformation and rumors. But always they are organizing around information.

People also work with whatever relationships the system allows, often going around the system to make critical connections. Most people know which relationships would bolster their effectiveness, although this awareness may be voiced only as complaints. And as they do their work and make decisions, employees reference the organizational identity that they see and feel—the organization's norms, unspoken expectations, the values that get rewarded.

When errors or problems occur, the real work is to look into the domains of self-organization and determine what's going on at this subterranean level. In organizations, problems show up in behaviors, processes, or structures. Once we diagnose the problem, our collective practice has been to substitute new behaviors, new structures, new processes for the problematic elements. But this seldom works. The problems that we see in organizations are artifacts of much deeper dynamics occurring in the domains of information, relationships, or identity. If we can inquire at this deeper level, if we can inquire into the dynamic heart of organizing, both the problem and the solution will be discovered.

We observed the power of inquiring into these depths in a DuPont chemical plant in Belle, West Virginia. Safety had been a major focus for many years, addressed in many different ways. They had moved from eighty-three recordable injuries to none. But after more than a year with no recordable injuries, three minor personal accidents occurred within a few months. The leadership team knew from past experience that the solution to their safety problems did not lie in new regulations. Instead, they examined the organization in terms of these originating dynamics of identity, information, and relationships. What were they, as leaders, trying to accomplish? Did they still believe in their principles? How were their relationships with one another? Did everyone still have access to all information?

These leaders could have responded in more traditional ways. They could have initiated disciplinary action, more regulations, safety training classes, or increased supervision. Instead, they questioned themselves more deeply and noted that because of several new members, they were no longer guided by the same shared clarity about safety. The re-creation of that clarity restored them to superior levels of safety performance.

If self-organization already exists in organizations—if people are naturally self-organizing—then the challenge for leaders is how to create the conditions that more effectively support this capacity. They do this by attending to what is available in the domains of information, relationships, and identity.

Leaders in Self-organizing Organizations

What do leaders do in self-organizing organizations? As their organizations move toward a mode of operating that seems to exclude most traditional activities of planning and control, is there a role for leaders? Absolutely. Leaders are an essential requirement for the move toward self—organization. This is not laissez-faire management disguised as new biology. Given existing hierarchies, only leaders can commit their organizations to this path. But their focus shifts dramatically from what has occupied them in the past. In our work, we have observed many of the pleasures and perils of leaders on this path. We also are aware of some of the siren calls that seem to threaten the resolve of even the clearest of leaders.

The path of self-organization can never be known ahead of time. There are no prescribed stages or models. "The road is your footsteps, nothing else," as the South American poet Machados wrote. Therefore, leaders begin with a strong *intention*, not a set of action plans. (Plans do emerge, but locally, from responses to needs and contingencies.) Leaders also must have confidence in the organization's intelligence. The future is unknown, but they believe the system is talented enough to organize in whatever ways the future requires.

This faith in the organization's ability and intelligence will be sorely tested. When there are failures, pressures from the outside, or employee problems, it is easy to retreat to more traditional structures and solutions. As one manager describes it: "When things aren't going well, we've had to resist the temptation to fall back to the *perceived* safety of our old, rigid structures. But we know that the growth, the creativity, the opening up, the energy improves only if we hold ourselves at the edge of chaos."

The path of self-organization offers ample tests for leaders to discover how much they really trust their employees. Can employees make wise decisions? Can they deal with sensitive information? Can they talk to the community or government regulators? Employees earn trust, but leaders create the circumstances in which such trust can be earned.

Because dependency runs so deep in most organizations these days, employees often have to be encouraged to exercise initiative and explore new areas of competence. Not only do leaders have to let go and watch as employees figure out their own solutions, but they also have to shore up their self-confidence and encourage them to do more. And leaders need to refrain from taking credit for their employees' good work—not always an easy task.

While self-organization calls us to very different ideas and forms of organizing, how else can we create the resilient, intelligent, fast, and flexible organizations that we require? How else can we succeed in organizing in the accelerating pace of our times except by realizing that organizations are living systems? This is not an easy shift, changing one's model of the way the world organizes. It is work that will occupy most of us for the rest of our careers. But the future pulls us toward these new understandings with an insistent and compelling call.

The Paradox and Promise of Community

with Myron Rogers

We human beings have a great need for one another. As described by the West African writer and teacher Malidoma Somé, we have "an instinct of community." However, this instinct to be together is devolving into growing fragmentation and separation. We experience increasing ethnic wars, community battle grounds, and self-serving special interest groups.

We are using the instinct of community to separate and protect us from one another, rather than creating a global culture of diverse yet interwoven communities. We search for those most like us in order to protect ourselves from the rest of society. Clearly, we cannot get to a future worth inhabiting through these separating paths. Our great task is to rethink our understandings of community so that we can move from the closed protectionism of current forms to an openness and embrace of the planetary community.

It is ironic that in the midst of this proliferation of specialty islands, we live surrounded by communities that know how to connect to others through their diversity, communities that succeed in creating sustainable relationships over long periods of time. These communities are the webs of relationships called *ecosystems*. Everywhere in nature, communities of diverse species live together in ways that support both the individual and the entire system. As they spin these systems into existence, new capabilities and talents emerge from the process of being together. These systems teach that the instinct of community is not peculiar to humans but is found everywhere in life, from microbes to the most complex species. They also teach that the way in which individuals weave themselves into ecosystems is quite paradoxical. This paradox can be a great teacher to us humans.

Life takes form as individuals that immediately reach out to create systems of relationships. These individuals and systems arise from two seemingly conflicting forces: the absolute need for individual freedom, and the unequivocal need for relationships. In human society, we struggle with the tension between these two forces. But in nature, successful examples of this paradox abound and reveal surprising treasures of insight. It is possible to create resilient and adaptive communities that welcome our diversity as well as our membership.

Life's first imperative is that it must be free to create itself. One biological definition of life is that something is alive if it has the capacity to create itself. Life begins with this primal freedom to create, the capacity for self-determination. An individual creates itself with a boundary that distinguishes it from others. Every individual and species is a different solution for how to live here. This freedom gives rise to the boundless diversity of the planet.

As an individual makes its way in the world, it exercises its freedom continuously. It is free to decide what to notice, what to invest with meaning. It is free to decide what its reaction will be, whether it will change or not. This freedom is so much a part of life that biologists Humberto Maturana and Francisco Varela advise that we can never direct a living system—we can only hope to get its attention. Life accepts only partners, not bosses, because self-determination is its very root of being.

Life's second great imperative propels individuals out from themselves to search for community. Life is systems seeking; there is the need to be in relationship, to be connected to others. When biologist Lynn Margulis notes that *independence* is not a concept that explains the living world, this means that it's only a political concept we've made up. Individuals cannot survive alone. They move out continuously to discover what relationships they require, what relationships are possible.

Evolution progresses from these new relationships, not from the harsh and lonely dynamics of survival of the fittest. Species that decide to ignore relationships, that act in greedy and rapacious ways, simply die off. If we look at the evolutionary record, it is cooperation that increases over time. This cooperation is spawned from a fundamental recognition that nothing can exist without the other, that it is only in relationship that one can be fully one's self. The instinct of community is everywhere in life.

As systems form, the paradox of individualism and connectedness becomes clearer. Individuals are figuring out how to be together in ways that support themselves. Yet these individuals remain astutely aware of their neighbors and local environmental conditions. They do not act from a blinding instinct for self-preservation. Nor do they act as passive recipients of someone else's demands. They are never forced to change by others or the environment. But as they choose to change, the "other" is a major influence on their individual decisions. The community is held in the awareness of the individual as that individual exercises its freedom to respond.

When an individual changes, its neighbors take notice and decide how they will respond. Over time, individuals become so intermeshed in this process of coevolving that it becomes impossible to distinguish the boundary between self and other, or self and environment. There is a continual exchange of information and energy between all neighbors, and a continuous process of change and adaptation everywhere in the system. And another paradox, it is these individual changes that contribute to the overall health and stability of the entire system.

As a system forms from such coevolutionary processes, the new system provides a level of stability and protection that was not available when individuals were isolated. And new capacities emerge in individuals and the system overall. Members develop new talents and new abilities as they work out relationships with others. Both individuals and systems grow in skill and complexity. Communities increase the capacity and complexity of life over time.

These complex networks of relationships offer very different possibilities for thinking about self and other. The very idea of boundaries changes profoundly. Rather than being a self-protective wall, boundaries become the place of meeting and exchange. We usually think of these edges as the means to define separateness, defining what's inside and what's outside. But in living systems, boundaries are something quite different. They are the place where new relationships take form, an important place of exchange and growth as an individual chooses to respond to another. As connections proliferate and the system weaves itself into existence, it becomes difficult to interpret boundaries as defenses, or even as markers of where one individual ends.

Human communities are no different from the rest of life. We form our communities from these same two needs—the need for self-determination and the need for one another. But in modern society, we have difficulty embracing the inherent paradox of these needs. We reach to satisfy one at the expense of the other. Very often the price of belonging to a community is to forfeit one's individual autonomy. Communities form around specific standards, doctrines, traditions. Individuals are required to conform, to obey, to serve "the greater good" of the community. Thus inclusion exacts a high price, that of our individual self-expression. With the loss of personal autonomy, diversity not only disappears but also becomes a major management problem. The community spends more and more energy on new ways to exert control over individuals through endlessly proliferating policies, standards, and doctrines.

The price that communities pay for this conformity is exhausting, and, for its members, it is literally deadly. Life requires the honoring of its two great needs, not one. In seeking to be a community member, we cannot abandon our need for self-expression. In the most restrictive communities, our need for freedom creeps in around the edges or moves us out of the community altogether. We modify our look and clothing; we create cliques that support our particular manner of being; we form splinter groups; we leave the physical community; we disagree over doctrine and create warring schisms. These behaviors demonstrate the unstoppable need for self-creation, even while we crave the support of others.

Particularly in the West, and in response to this too-demanding price of belonging, we move toward isolationism in order to defend our individual freedom. We choose a life lived alone in order for it to be *our* life. We give up the meaningful life that can only be discovered in relationship with others for a meaningless life that at least we think is ours. What we can see from our pursuit of individualism is the terrible price exacted for such independence. We end up in vacant places, overwhelmed by loneliness and the emptiness of life.

It seems that whenever we bargain with life and seek to satisfy only one of its two great needs, the result is a lifelessness. We must live within the paradox; life does not allow us to choose sides. Our communities must support our individual freedom as a means to community health and resiliency. And individuals must acknowledge their neighbors and make choices based on the desire to be in relationship with them as a means to their own health and resiliency.

At first glance, the World Wide Web seems to be a source of new communities. But these groups do not embrace the paradox of community. The great potential of a world connected electronically is being used to create stronger boundaries that keep us isolated from one another. Through the Web, we can seek relationships with others who are exactly like us. We are responding to our instinct of community, but we form highly specialized groups in the image of ourselves, groups that reinforce our separateness from the rest of society.

We are not asked to contribute our uniqueness, only our sameness. We are not asked to encounter, much less celebrate, the fact that we need one another's gifts. We can turn off our computers the moment we're confronted with the discomfort of diversity. Such specialized, self-reflecting networks lead to as much destructiveness of the individual as any dictatorial, doctrine-based organization. In neither type of group are we asked to explore our individualism while being in relationship with others who remain different. In neither type of group are we honoring the paradox of freedom and community.

In human communities, the conditions of freedom and connectedness are kept vibrant by focusing on what's going on in the heart of the community rather than being fixated on the forms and rules of the community. What called us together? What did we believe was possible together that was not possible alone? What did we hope to bring forth by linking with others? These questions invite in both our individuality and our desire for relationships. If we stay with these questions and don't try to structure relationships through policies and doctrines, we can create communities that thrive in the paradox.

Clarity of purpose at the core of the community changes the entire nature of relationships within that community. These communities do not ask people to forfeit their freedom as a condition of belonging. They avoid the magnetic pull of proscribing behaviors and beliefs, they avoid becoming doctrinaire and dicta-torial, they stay focused on what they're trying to create together, and diversity flourishes within them. Belonging together is defined by a shared sense of purpose, not by shared beliefs about specific behaviors. The call of purpose attracts individuals but does not require them to shed their uniqueness. Staying centered on what the work is together, rather than on single identities, trans-forms the tension of belonging and individuality into energetic and resilient communities.

In our own work, we have seen these communities in schools, towns, and organizations. They create themselves around a shared intent and some basic principles about how to be together. They do not get into a prescriptive role with one another. They do found their community not on directives but on desire. They know why they are together, and they have agreed on the conditions of how to be together. And, very importantly, these conditions are kept to a minimum of specificity.

One of the most heartening examples we've encountered is a junior high school that operates as a robust community of students, faculty, and staff by agreeing that all behaviors and decisions are based on three rules and just three rules. These are "Take care of yourself. Take care of each other. Take care of this place." These rules are sufficient to keep them connected and focused, and they are open enough to allow for diverse and individual responses to any situation. (The fact that this worked so well in a junior high environment should make us all sit up and take notice!) The principal reported that after the building had to be evacuated during a rainstorm, he returned last into the building and was greeted by eight hundred pairs of shoes in the lobby. The children had decided, in that particular circumstance, how to "take care of this place."

We have also seen businesses and large cities rally themselves around a renewed and clear sense of collective purpose. A chemical plant becomes clear that it wants to contribute to the safety of the globe by its safe manufacturing processes; a city determines that it wants to be a place where children can thrive. These are clarifying messages to hold at the core of the community. This clarity helps every individual to exercise his or her freedom to decide how best to contribute to this deeply shared purpose. Diversity and unique gifts become a contribution rather than an issue of compliance or deviance. Problems of diversity disappear as we focus on contribution to a shared purpose rather than the legislation of correct behavior.

Other problematic behaviors also disappear when a community knows its heart, its purpose for being together. Boundaries between self and other, who's outside and who's inside, get weaker and weaker. The deep interior clarity we share frees us to look for partners who can help us achieve our purpose. We reach out farther and welcome in more diverse voices because we learn that they are helpful contributors to what we are trying to birth. The manager of the chemical plant mentioned earlier said that he no longer knew where his plant boundaries were and that it was unimportant to try to define them. Instead, the plant was in more and more relationships with people in the community, the government, suppliers, foreign competitors, churches, and schoolchildren—all of whom contributed to the workers' desire to become one of the safest and highest-quality plants in the world, a desire that they achieved.

Today, so many of our communities and the institutions that serve them are lost because they lack clarity about why they are together. Few schools know what the community wants of them; the same is true for health care, government, the military. We no longer agree on what we want these institutions to provide, because we no longer are members of communities that know why they are together. Most of us don't feel like we are members of a community; we just live or work next to each other. The great missing conversation is about why and how we might be together.

But as lost as we are, there is hope. Even in our fractured communities, people continue to talk together about questions of identity and meaning. What do they want in their children's school? How should development be handled? What do we offer to new immigrants? No matter the topic, these conversations involve fundamental questions of "Who are we?" and "What matters?" The problem is that these are private conversations occurring around kitchen tables, in parking lots and restaurants. Seldom are these critical community questions asked in institutions or the broader community. Yet these *are* the essential questions from which all communities give birth to the institutions that are meant to serve them—schools, agencies, churches, governments.

When we don't answer these questions as a community, when we have no agreements about why we belong together, the institutions we create to serve us become battlegrounds that serve no one. All energy goes into warring agendas, new regulations, stronger protective measures against those we dislike and fear. We look for ourselves in these institutions and can't find anyone we recognize. We grow more demanding and less satisfied. Our institutions dissipate into incoherence and impotence. They only serve us as mirrors that reflect back to us the lack of cohering agreements at the heart of our community. Without these agreements about why we belong together, we can never develop institutions that make any sense at all. In the absence of these agreements, our instinct of community leads us to a community of "me," not a community of "we."

Most public meetings, although originating from a democratic ideal, serve only to increase our separation from one another. Agendas and processes try to honor our differences but end up increasing our distance. They are "public hearings" where nobody is listening and everyone is demanding air time. Communities aren't created from such processes—they are destroyed by the increasing fear and separation that these processes engender. Such public processes also generate the destructive power dynamics that emerge when people feel isolated and unheard.

We don't need more public hearings. We need much more public listening, in processes where we come together and commit to staying together long enough to discover those ideas and issues that are significant to each of us. We don't have to interpret an event or issue the same, but we do have to share a sense that it is significant. In our experience, as soon as people realize that others around them, no matter how different, share this sense of significance, they quickly move into new relationships with one another. They become able to work together, not because they have won anyone over to their view but because they have connected in a deeper place, a place we identify as the organizing center or heart of the community.

We *can* reach entirely new levels of possibility together, possibilities that are not available from soap box rhetoric. To achieve this, we need to begin these conversations about purpose and shared significance and commit to staying in them. As we stay in the conversation, people start to work together rather than convince each other of who has more of the truth. We *are* capable of creating wonderful and vibrant communities when we discover what dreams of possibility we share. And always, those dreams become much greater than anything that was ever available when we were isolated from each other. The history of most community-organizing and great social change movements can be traced back to such conversations, conversations among friends and strangers who discovered a shared sense of what was important to them.

As we create communities from the cohering center of shared significance, from a mutual belief in why we belong together, we will discover what is already visible everywhere around us in living systems. People's great creativity and diversity, our desire for contribution and relationships, blossom when the heart of our community is clear and beckoning, and when we refrain from cluttering our paths with proscriptions and demands. The future of community is best taught to us by life.

Relying on Human Goodness

We have a great need to remember the fact of human goodness. Today, human goodness seems like an outrageous "fact." Every moment we are confronted with mounting evidence of the great harm we so easily do to one another.

We are bombarded with global images of genocide, dislocations caused by ethnic hatred, and stories of individual violence committed daily in communities around the world. The word *evil* comes easily to our lips to explain these terrible behaviors.

And in our day-to-day lives, we are directly confronted by people who are angry, deceitful, and interested only in their own needs. In organizations and communities, we struggle to find ways to work together amidst so much anger, distrust and pettiness.

But I know that the only path to creating more harmonious and effective workplaces and communities is if we can turn to one another and depend on one another. We cannot cope, much less create, in this increasingly fast and turbulent world, without each other. We must search for human goodness.

There is no substitute for human creativity, human caring, human will. We can be incredibly resourceful, imaginative, and open-hearted. We can do the impossible, learn and change quickly, and extend instant compassion to those suffering from natural and political disasters.

And these are not behaviors we only use occasionally. If you look at your daily life, how often do you figure out an answer to a problem, or find a slightly better way of doing something, or extend yourself to someone in need? Very few people go through their days as robots, doing only repetitive tasks, never noticing that anybody else is nearby. Take a moment to look around at your colleagues and neighbors, and you'll see the same behaviors—people trying to be useful, trying to make some small contribution, trying to help someone else.

We have forgotten what we're capable of and let our worst natures rise to the surface. I believe we got into this sorry state partly because, for too long, we've been treating people as machines. We've tried to force people into tiny boxes, called roles and job descriptions. We've told people what to do and how they should behave. We've believed we could "reengineer" organizations to be efficient machines and treated people as replaceable parts in the machinery of production.

After so many years of being bossed around, of working within confining roles, of unending reorganization, reengineering, downsizing, mergers and power plays, most people are exhausted, cynical, and focused only on self-protection. Who wouldn't be? But it's important to remember that *we created* these negative and demoralized people. We created them by relying on organizing processes that discount and deny our best human capacities.

If you look around at most organizations and communities, people are still being kept in boxes. They are not invited to contribute, to create, or to care about each other. Instead, it's assumed that people must be policed into good behavior. Endless policies and laws attempt to make us behave properly. Yet very few people tolerate this disrespect and constraint on their personal freedom. We become rebellious, hostile, cynical—or we shut down and look as if we died on the job. Whole cultures and generations of people become deadened by coercion, but underneath, the apathy and withdrawal still live human spirits that aspire to live lives of their own choosing.

It is time to become passionate about what's best in us and to create organizations that welcome in our creativity, contribution, and compassion. We do this by using processes that bring us together to talk to one another, listen to one another's stories, reflect together on what we're learning as we do our work. We do this by developing relationships of trust, where we do what we say, where we speak truthfully, where we refuse to act from petty self-interest. These processes and relationships have already been developed by many courageous companies, leaders, and facilitators. Many pioneers have created processes and organizations that depend on human capacity and know how to evoke our very best.

In my experience, people everywhere are longing for new ways of working together, and for more harmonious relationships. We know we need to work together, because daily we are overwhelmed by problems that we can't solve alone. People want to help. We want to contribute. We want to feel hopeful.

As leaders, as neighbors, as colleagues, it is time to turn to one another, to engage in the intentional search for human goodness. In our meetings and deliberations, we can reach out and invite in those we have excluded. We can recognize that no one person or leader has the answer, that we need every-body's creativity to find our way through this strange new world. We can act from the certainty that most people want to care about others and invite them to step forward with their compassion. We can realize that "you can't hate someone whose story you know."

We *are* our only hope for creating a future worth working for. We can't go it alone, we can't get there without each other, and we can't create it without relying anew on our fundamental and precious human goodness.

The Best in Art and Life

Roger Rosenblatt

The best in art and life
comes from a center
something urgent and powerful
an ideal or emotion
that insists
    on its being.

From that insistence
a shape emerges
    and creates its structure out of passion.

If you begin with a structure,
you have to make up the passion,

    and that's very hard to do.

Note: Prose text redone as a poem by Meg Wheatley.

Leadership
We Make the Road by Walking

Goodbye, Command and Control
Relying on Everyone's Creativity
Bringing Life to Organizational Change
Working with Life's Dynamics in School Systems
When Change Is Out of Our Control
Leadership in Turbulent Times Is Spiritual

These essays focus specifically on leadership. They apply living systems theory to essential challenges, from how leaders can avoid grasping for control, to how we lead enduring change that motivates people, to how we strengthen our resolve and peacefulness.

It is more a matter of believing the good than of seeing it as the fruit of our efforts.

—Chuang Tzu, China, third-century B.C.E.

Goodbye, Command and Control

Old ways die hard. Amid all the evidence that our world is radically changing, we retreat to what has worked in the past. These days, leaders respond to increasing uncertainty by defaulting to command and control. Power has been taken back to the top of most major corporations, governments, and organizations, and workers have been consigned to routine, exhausting work.

The dominance of command and control is having devastating impacts. There has been a dramatic increase in worker disengagement, no one is succeeding at solving problems, and leaders are being scapegoated and fired.

Most people associate command and control leadership with the military. Years ago, I worked for the U.S. Army chief of staff, General Gordon Sullivan. I, like most people, thought I'd see command-and-control leadership there. The great irony is that the military learned long ago that, if you want to win, you have to engage the intelligence of everyone involved in the battle. I've heard many military commanders state that "if you have to order a soldier to do something, then you've failed as a leader." The army had a visual reminder of the failure of command and control when, years ago, they developed the new tanks and armored vehicles that could travel at speeds of fifty miles an hour. During the first Gulf War, there were several instances when troops took off on their own and sped across the desert at this unparalleled speed. However, according to army doctrine, tanks and armored vehicles always had to be accompanied by a third vehicle that is literally called Command and Control. This vehicle could only travel at twenty miles an hour. (They corrected this problem.)

For me, this is a familiar image—people in the organization ready and willing to do good work, wanting to contribute their ideas, ready to take responsibility, and leaders holding them back, insisting that they wait for decisions or instructions. The result is dispirited employees and leaders wondering why no one takes responsibility or gets engaged anymore. In these troubled, uncertain times, we don't need more command and control; we need better means to engage everyone's intelligence in solving challenges and crises as they arise.

We do know how to create workplaces that are flexible, smart, and resilient. We have known for more than half a century that self-managed teams are far more productive than any other form of organizing. There is a clear correlation between participation and productivity; in fact, productivity gains in truly self-managed work environments are *at minimum 35 percent higher* than in traditionally managed organizations. And for years, people in all types of organizations have asked for more autonomy, insisting that they can make smarter changes than those delivered from on high. People need more autonomy in their work, and there is strong evidence that such participation leads to the adaptability and productivity leaders crave.

With so much evidence supporting the benefits of participation, why isn't every organization using self-managed teams to cope with turbulence? Instead, organizations are cluttered with control mechanisms that paralyze employees and leaders alike. Where have all these policies, procedures, protocols, laws, and regulations come from? And why do we keep creating more, even as we suffer from the terrible consequences of overcontrol?

One answer is that, over the years, leaders consistently have chosen power rather than productivity. They would rather be in control than have the organization work at optimal efficiency. And now there's another belief surfacing: When risk runs high, power must be wielded by only a few people. Just the opposite is true. Reflective leaders, including those in the military, have learned that the higher the risk, the more we need everyone's commitment and intelligence. In holding onto power and refusing to distribute decision making, leaders have created unwieldy, Byzantine systems that only increase risk and irresponsibility. We never effectively control people or situations with these systems, we only succeed in preventing intelligent work.

In the midst of so much fear, it's important to remember something we all know: People organize together to accomplish more, not less. Behind every organizing impulse is a hope that by joining with others we can accomplish something important that we could not accomplish alone. And this impulse to organize in order to accomplish more is not only true of humans but found in all living systems. Every living thing seeks to create a world in which it can thrive. Organization is a naturally occurring phenomenon. The world organizes to find its own effectiveness. And so do people in organizations.

As a living system self-organizes, it develops shared understanding of what's important, what's acceptable behavior, what actions are required, and how these actions will get done. It develops channels of communication, networks of workers, and complex physical structures. And as the system develops, new capacities emerge. Looking at this list of what a self-organizing system creates leads to the realization that the system can do for itself most of what leaders have felt was necessary to do to it.

Whenever we deny life's self-organizing capacity, leaders must struggle to change these systems by imposition. They tinker with the incentives, reshuffle the pieces, change a part, or retrain a group. But these efforts are doomed to fail, and nothing will make them work. What is required is a shift in how we think about organizing. Effective organization occurs as people see what needs to happen, apply their experience and perceptions to the issue, find those who can help them, and use their own creativity to invent solutions. This process is going on right now in organizations, in spite of efforts at control. People are exercising initiative from a desire to contribute, displaying the creativity common to all life. Can we recognize the self-organizing behaviors in organizations?

Can we learn to support people and leave behind fear-based approaches to leadership?

Belief in People

Leaders who have used more participative, self-organizing approaches tell of how astonished they are by the capacity, energy, creativity, commitment, and even love they receive from people in their organizations. In the past, they assumed that most people were there for the money, that they didn't care about the whole enterprise, that they were narrowly focused, perhaps self-serving.

No leader would openly voice these assumptions, but most leader behaviors reveal these beliefs. Does the leader promote his or her vision as the means to energize the organization? Does the organization keep changing incentives to motivate employees? Does the organization keep reorganizing, pushing new designs and plans on people as the route to greater productivity? How often are employees trusted to make decisions that directly affect their work?

Every so often, in a moment of truth, we realize the conflict between our behaviors and our deeper knowledge. As one manager of a Fortune 100 company said: "I know in my heart that when people are driving into work, they're not thinking, 'How can I mess things up today? How can I give my boss a hard time?' No one is driving here with that intent, but we then act as if we believed that. We're afraid to give them any slack."

Enough people drive to work wondering how they can get something done *despite the organization*—despite the political craziness, the bureaucratic nightmares, the mindless procedures blocking their way. Those leaders who have used participation and self-organization have witnessed the inherent desire that most people have to contribute to their organizations. The commitment and energy resident in people takes leaders by surprise. But it's quite predictable. As leaders honor and trust the people who work with them, they unleash star- tlingly high levels of contribution and creativity.

Coherence, Not Control

If we think of organizations as living systems capable of self-organizing, then how do we think about change in these systems? The strategy for change becomes simpler and more localized. We need to encourage the creativity that lives throughout the organization, but keep local solutions localized. Too many change efforts fail when an innovation that people have invented in one area of the organization is rolled out through the entire organization. *This attempt to replicate success actually destroys local initiative.* It denies the creativity of every- one else. All living systems change all the time as they search for solutions. But they never act from some master plan. They tinker in their local environments, based on their intimate experience with conditions there, and their tinkering results in effective innovation. But only for them.

Information about what others have invented, what has worked elsewhere, can be very helpful to people elsewhere in the organization. These stories spark other's imagination, they help others become more insightful. However, no premade model can be imposed on people. The moment they leave home, where they were created, they become inspiration, not solutions.

Localized change activity does not mean that the organization spins off wildly in all directions. If people are clear about the purpose and real values of their organization, their individual tinkering will result in systemwide coherence. In organizations that know who they are and mean what they announce, people are free to create and contribute. A plurality of effective solutions emerges, each expressing a deeper coherence, an understanding of what this organiza- tion is trying to become.

Mort Meyerson, the former chairman of Perot Systems, said in an interview in *Fast Company* magazine several years ago that the primary task of being a leader is to make sure that the organization knows itself. That is, the leader's task is to call people together often, so that everyone gains clarity about what they're doing, who they've become and how they're changing as they do their work. This includes information available from customers, markets, history, mistakes. A good leader supports a continuous conversation about organizational identity and how it is changing as it does its work in a changing world.

Organizations that are clear at their core work from congruence, not coercion. People feel free to explore new activities, new ventures, and customers if they feel it makes sense for the organization. It is a strange and promising paradox: Clarity about who we are as an organization or team creates freedom for individual contributions. People exercise that freedom in service to the organization and, as they develop their capacity to respond and change, this becomes a capability of the whole organization.

As leaders ensure that the organization knows itself, that it's clear at its core, they must also learn to tolerate unprecedented levels of "messiness" at the edges. This constant tinkering, this localized hunt for solutions, never looks neat. Freedom and creativity always create diverse responses. If conformity is the goal, it will kill local initiative. Leaders have to be prepared to support diversity, to welcome surprise, to expect invention, to rely on highly contributing employees.

People always want to talk about what they do, what they see, how they can improve things, what they know about their customers. Supporting these conversations is an essential task of leaders. It's not about the leader developing the mission statement or employing experts to do a detailed analysis of market strategy. These activities, because they exclude more people than they include, never work as planned. When everyone in the organization understands the organization's identity and contributes (even in a small way) to enacting this, the result is high levels of commitment and capacity. As a leader supports the processes that help the organization know itself, the organization flourishes.

It's also notable that when we engage in meaningful conversations as an organization, and when we engage our customers, suppliers, community, and regulators in these conversations, everything changes. People develop new levels of trust for one another, they become more cooperative and forgiving. People stop being so arbitrary and demanding when they are part of the process, when they no longer have to dramatize their voice in order to get someone's attention.

Taking Action

Leaders put a premium on action. Organizations that have learned how to think together and that know themselves are filled with intelligent action. People are constantly taking initiative and making changes, often without asking or telling. Their individual freedom and creativity becomes a critical resource to the organization. Their local responsiveness translates into an agile and more adaptable organization overall.

But leaders need to know how to support self-organizing responses. People do not need the intricate directions, time lines, plans, and organization charts that are assumed to be necessary. These are not how people accomplish good work; they are what impede contributions. But people need a great deal from their leaders. They need information, access to one another, resources, trust, and follow-through. Leaders are necessary to foster experimentation, to help create connections across the organization, to feed the system with information from multiple sources—all while helping everyone stay clear on what we agreed we wanted to accomplish and who we wanted to be.

Most of us were raised in a culture that told us that the way to manage for excellence was to tell people exactly what they had to do and then make sure they did it. We learned to play master designer, assuming we could engineer people into perfect performance. But you can't direct people into excellence; you can only engage them enough so that they want to do excellent work. For example, in manufacturing plants that operate with near-perfect safety records for years at a time, these results are achieved because their workers are committed to safety. It becomes a personal mission. Government regulations are necessary parts of their system, but they never can spell out the route to perfect safety. That comes from hundreds and thousands of workers who understand their role in safety, who understand what contributes to safety, and who understand that it's up to them.

For all the unscripted events—an irate customer, a winter storm, a global crisis—we depend on individual initiative. Ultimately, we have to rely not on the procedure manuals but on people's intelligence and their commitment to doing the right thing. If they are acting by rote or regimen, they've lost the capacity for excellence. Imposed control only breeds passivity, resistance, resentment, and irresponsibility.

Quick Fixes Are an Oxymoron

Self-organization is a long-term exploration requiring enormous self-awareness and support. This is true partially because it represents such a fundamentally different way of thinking about organization, and partially because all changes in organization take much longer than we want to acknowledge. If leaders would learn anything from the past many years, it's that there are no quick fixes. For most organizations, meaningful change is at least a three- to five-year process— although this seems impossibly long. Yet multiyear change efforts are the hard reality we must face. These things take time. How long, for instance, has your organization been struggling with quality, with excellence? How long has it been searching for the right organizational design? How many years have you been working to create effective teams? Jack Welch, for one, understood that it would take at least ten years to develop the capacities of GE's people. In the late 1980s, that was a radical insight and a startling commitment.

Most CEOs don't want to squeeze their organizations for short-term profitability or shortsighted outcomes that don't endure. Most leaders resent the focus on quarterly or monthly measures of success. Legacy is an important issue for many leaders—a deep desire for their work to mean something, to endure beyond their tenure. Leaders, too, have suffered from the terrible destruction visited on many organizations. A senior executive of a major industrial firm, speaking for many, said, "I've just been told to destroy what I spent twenty years creating." Who among us wants to end a career with that realization?

But if we are to develop organizations of greater and enduring capacity, we have to turn to the people of our organization. We have to learn how to encourage the creativity and commitment that they wanted to express when they first joined the organization. We have to learn how to get past the distress and cynicism that's been created in the past several years and use our best talents to figure out how to reengage people in the important work of organizing.

The Leader's Journey

Whenever humans need to change a deeply structured belief system, everything in life is called into question—relationships with loved ones, children, colleagues, authority, and major institutions. A group of senior leaders, reflecting on the changes they had experienced, commented that the higher you are in the organization, the more change is required of you personally. Those who have led their organizations into new ways often say that the most important change was personal. Nothing would have changed in their organizations if they hadn't changed.

All this seems true to me, but I think the story is more complex. Leaders managing difficult personal transitions are also engaged in many other changes in the organization. They are supporting teams, fostering collaboration and more participative processes, introducing new ways of thinking. They are setting a great many things in motion simultaneously within the organization. Some work, some don't, but the climate for experimentation is evident. A change here elicits a response there, which calls for a new idea, which elicits yet another response. It's an intricate exchange and coevolution, and it's nearly impossible to look back and name any single change as the cause of all the others. In this way, organizational change is a dance, not a forced march.

Leaders experience their own personal change most intensely, and so I think they report on this as the key process. But what I observe is far more interesting. In the end, we can't define a simple list of activities that were responsible for the organization shifting, and we certainly can't replicate anyone else's process for success. But we can encourage the experimentation and tinkering, the constant feedback and learning, and the wonderful sense of camaraderie that emerges as everyone gets engaged in making the organization work better than ever before, even in the most difficult of circumstances.

Enduring Organizations

I believe there is one principle that should be embraced by all organizations as they move into the future, and that is endurability. How can we last over time? What about us is worth sustaining long-term? This focus flies in the face of current fashion. Our infatuation with "virtual" organizations, outsourcing, and short-term contracts misses an important truth: We cannot create an organization that means something to its people if that organization has no life beyond the next project or contract. We cannot promise people, for instance, only a few months or years of employment and expect the kind of energy and commitment that I've described.

In response to the grave uncertainty we feel about the future—since we can't predict markets, products, customers, governments, or anything—we decide not to promise anything to anyone. Too many leaders are saying, in effect, "We don't know what the future will be or how to manage this uncertainty, so let's think of our employees as negotiable commodities." What they've really said is "Let's buy flexibility by giving up loyalty."

Commitment and loyalty are essential in human relationships. So how can we pretend we don't need them at work? The real issue is that we don't know how to engage people's loyalty and yet maintain the flexibility we require. But leaders should be searching for creative answers to this dilemma, not ignoring it by settling on these nonsolutions of short-term or temporary work. The organizations that people love to work in are those that have a sense of history, identity, and purpose. Companies that have stood for something in the past, that stand for something now, provide compelling reasons for people to work hard. They work to ensure that these organizations move well into the future.

Relying on Everyone's Creativity

I am always happily surprised by how impossible it is to extinguish the human spirit. People who had been given up for dead in their organizations find new energy and become great innovators once conditions change and they feel welcomed back.

Plant workers who worked for thirty years under an autocratic manager reawaken as creative contributors when a new, participative leader arrives. A professor who'd been holed up in his office for many years waiting for retirement becomes a national speaker representing his university's new initiative because he cares about it so deeply.

How do we acknowledge that everyone is a potential innovator? How can we evoke the innate human need to create?

The capacity to create and adapt is universal. Scientists keep discovering more species; they don't know if there are ten million or fifty million species. Yet each one is an embodiment of innovations that worked. Except us humans, who seem to resist change. Could this possibly be true? Are we the only species—out of so many millions—that digs in its heels and resists? Or perhaps all those other creatures simply went to better training programs on "Innovation for Competitive Advantage."

Many years ago, Joel Barker popularized the notion of paradigms or worldviews, those beliefs and assumptions through which we see the world and explain its processes. He stated that when something is impossible to achieve with one worldview, it can be surprisingly easy to accomplish with a new one. I have found this to be delightfully true. As we understand people and organizations as living systems, filled with the innovative dynamics characteristic of all life, many intractable problems become solvable. Perhaps the most powerful example in my own work is that it is possible to create successful organizational change if you start with the assumption that people, like all life, are creative and good at change. Once we stop treating organizations and people as machines and move to the paradigm of living systems, organizational change is not a problem. Using this new worldview, it is possible to create organizations rich in people who are capable of adapting as needed, who are alert to changes in their environment, who are able to innovate strategically. It is possible to work with the innovative potential that exists in all of us and to engage that potential to solve meaningful problems.

Western culture developed a strangely negative and unfamiliar view of humans as machines. This resulted in a collective view of us as passive, unemotional, fragmented, incapable of self-motivation, disinterested in meaningful questions or good work.

But the twenty-first-century world of complex systems is no place for these disabling and dispiriting images. We are confronted daily by events and outcomes that shock us and for which we have no answers. The complexity of modern systems cannot be understood by our old ways of separating problems, or scapegoating individuals, or rearranging the boxes on an org chart. In a complex system, it is impossible to find simple causes that explain our problems or to know who to blame. A messy tangle of relationships has given rise to these unending crises. To understand this new world of continuous change and intimately connected systems, we need new ways of understanding. Fortunately, life and its living systems offer great teachings on how to work in a world of continuous change and boundless creativity. And foremost among life's teachings is the recognition that human creativity and commitment are our greatest resources.

Some people still wonder if organizations *are* living systems. I don't engage in that question anymore, ever since I realized that the people working in organizations *are* alive. Therefore, they must respond to the same needs and conditions as any other living system. I personally don't require any other clarity. One gift of living systems is that these processes apply to individuals, to systems, to any size system. The dynamics of life are "scale-independent"—they are useful to explain what we see no matter how small or large the living system.

The new worldview of organizations as living systems offers many principles for leadership. Together they allow leaders to meet a great challenge—to create the conditions where human ingenuity can flourish.

Engage Creativity through Meaning

Every change, every burst of creativity, begins with the identification of a problem or opportunity that somebody finds meaningful. As soon as people become interested in an issue, their creativity is engaged. If we want people to be innovative, leaders must engage them in meaningful issues. The simplest way to discover what's meaningful is to notice what people talk about and where they spend their energy.

It doesn't help to listen to self-reports or to take the word of only a few people. Only by working inside a group or with an individual over time can we learn who they are and what attracts their attention. As we work together, *doing real work*, meaning always becomes visible. For example, what topics generate the most energy, positive or negative? What issues do people keep returning to? What stories do they tell over and over? No one can learn this from outside the group, observing behaviors or collecting data in traditional ways. We have to be there, working.

In any group, we need to expect to hear multiple and diverging interpretations. It helps to put ideas, proposals, and issues on the table as *experiments to see what's meaningful* to people rather than as recommendations for what *should* be meaningful to them.

Here's one of my favorite stories of how we never know what others find meaningful: A group of health care professionals started a campaign to distribute child car seats to low-income parents. They assumed that these would be welcome items, but after several months they noted that the car seats weren't being used. They responded by offering training programs in the use of these seats, including statistics on how they prevented infant deaths. But to no avail. Finally, they sat down with parents in the community and asked them why they weren't using them. To their surprise, they learned that for these parents from a non-Western culture, strapping a child into a car seat was an invitation to God to cause a car accident. Car seats didn't protect their children from death. Instead, they invoked the wrath of God.

From many surprises like this one, I've learned it's more useful to cultivate curiosity rather than certainty. It's not easy to stay open, but when we listen for diversity rather than expecting agreement, we can learn that no two people see the world exactly the same.

Depend on Diversity

Life relies on diversity to give it the possibility of adapting to changing conditions. If a system becomes too homogenous, it becomes vulnerable to environmental shifts. If one form is dominant, and that form no longer works when the environment shifts, the entire system can collapse. Where there is diversity in an organization, innovative solutions are created all the time, just because different people do things differently. When the environment changes and demands a different approach, we can count on the fact that somebody is already practicing that new solution. Almost always, in a diverse organization, the solution the organization needs is already being practiced somewhere in that system. If leaders fail to encourage diverse ways of doing things, they destroy the system's capacity to adapt. Organizations need people experimenting with many different ways, just in case. And when the environment demands change, we can look inside the organizations to find those solutions that have already been prepared for us by our colleagues.

There is another reason why diversity is critical to an organization's ability to innovate and adapt. Organizations and societies are so complex, filled with so many intertwining and diverging interests, personalities, and issues, that nobody can confidently represent anybody else's point of view. Our markets and our organizations behave as "units of one." There is no possibility that we can adequately represent anybody else. But there is a simple solution to this dilemma. We can ask people for their unique perspective. We can invite them to share the world as they see it. We can listen for the differences. And we can trust that with curiosity, we will create a much richer mosaic from our unique perspectives.

Involve Everybody Who Cares

Working with many kinds of organizations over the past several years, I've learned the hard way that broad-based participation is not optional. As leaders, we have no choice but to figure out how to invite in everybody who is going to be affected by change. Those that we fail to invite into the creation process will surely and always show up as resistors and saboteurs. But I haven't become insistent on participation just to avoid resistance or to get people to support my efforts. It's because no one person is smart enough to design anything for the whole system. No one of us these days can know what will work inside the dense networks we call organizations. We can't see what's meaningful to people or even understand how they get their work done. We have no option but to invite them into the design process.

I know from experience that most people are very intelligent—they have figured out how to make things work when it seemed impossible; they have invented ways to get around roadblocks and dumb policies; they have created their own networks to support them and help them learn. But rarely is this visible to the organization until and unless we invite people in to participate in solution–creation processes. The complexity and density of organizations require that we engage the whole system so we can harvest the invisible intelligence that exists throughout the organization.

Fortunately, during the past ten years, pioneering work has been done on how to engage large numbers of people in creating innovation and strategy. Yet even in the presence of strong evidence for how well these processes work, most leaders still hesitate to venture down the participation path. Leaders have had so many bad experiences with participation that describing it as "not optional" seems like a death sentence. But we have to accept two simple truths: We can't force anybody to change, and no two people see the world the same way. We can only engage people in the change process from the beginning and see what's possible. If the issue is meaningful to them, they will become enthusiastic and bright advocates. If we want people's intelligence and support, we must welcome them as cocreators. People only support what they create.

Encourage Diversity as the Path to Unity

All change begins with a change in meaning. Yet we each see the world differently. Is it possible to develop a sense of shared meaning without denying our diversity? Are there ways that organizations can develop a shared sense of what's significant without forcing people to accept someone else's viewpoint?

There is a powerful paradox here. If we are willing to listen for diverse interpretations, we discover that our differing perceptions most often share a unifying center. As we become aware of this unity in diversity, it changes our relationships for the better. We recognize that through our diversity, we share a dream, or we share a sense of injustice. Then, magical things happen to our relationships. We open to each other as colleagues. Past hurts and negative histories get left behind. People step forward to work together. We don't hang back; we don't withdraw; we don't wait to be enticed. We actively seek each other out because the problem is important. The meaningfulness of the issue sounds louder than past grievances or difficulties. As we discover something whose importance we share, we want to work together.

I've been humbled to see how a group can come together as it recognizes its mutual interests. Working together becomes possible because they have discovered a shared meaning for the work that is strong enough to embrace them all. Held together in this center of meaning, people let go of many interpersonal difficulties, and work around traditional hindrances. They know they need each other. They are willing to struggle with relationships and figure out how to make them work because they realize this is the only path to achieving their aspirations.

Expect to Be Surprised by People's Contributions

Perhaps because of the study of human psychology, perhaps because we're just too busy to get to know each other, we have become a society that labels people in greater and greater detail. We know each other's personality types, leadership styles, syndromes, and neurotic behaviors. We are quick to assign people to a typology and then dismiss them, as if we really knew who they were. If we're trying to get something done in our organization, and things start going badly, we hunt for scapegoats to explain why it's not working. We notice only those who impede our good plans—all those "resistors," those stubborn and scared colleagues who cling to the past. We label ourselves also, but more generously, as "early adopters" or "cultural creatives."

In our crazed haste, we don't have time to get to know each other, to be curious about who a person is or why she or he is behaving a particular way. Listening to colleagues—their interpretations, their stories, what they find meaningful in their work—always transforms our relationships. The act of listening always brings us closer. We may not like the person or approve of their behavior, but if we listen, we move past the labels. Our "enemy" category shrinks in population. We notice another human being who has a reason for certain actions, who is trying to make some small contribution to our organization or community. The stereotypes that have divided us melt away and we discover that we want to work together. We realize that only by joining together will we be able to create the change we each want to see in the world.

Bringing Life to Organizational Change

with Myron Rogers

In the 1990s, surveys began reporting disappointing failures with organization change. CEOs reported that up to 75 percent of their organizational change efforts did not yield the promised results. These change efforts fail to produce what had been hoped for yet always produce a stream of unintended and unhelpful consequences. Leaders end up managing the impact of unwanted effects rather than the planned results that don't materialize.

Instead of enjoying the fruits of a redesigned production unit, the leader must manage the hostility and broken relationships created by the redesign. Instead of glorying in the new efficiencies produced by restructuring, the leader faces a burned-out and demoralized group of survivors. Instead of basking in a soaring stock price after a merger, leaders scramble frantically to get people to work together peaceably, let alone effectively.

In the search to understand so much failure, a lot of blame gets assigned. One health care executive commented, "We're under so much stress that all we do is look around the organization to find somebody we can shoot." (And the executive quoted is a nun!) It's become commonplace to say that people resist change, that the organization lacks the right people to move it into the future, that people no longer assume responsibility for their work, that people are too dependent, that all they do is whine.

Can we put a stop to all this slander and the ill will it's creating in our organizations? Most organizational change failures are the result of some deep misunderstandings of who people are and what's going on inside organizations. If we can clear up these misunderstandings, effectiveness and hope can return to our work. Successful organizational change is possible if we look at our organizational experience with new eyes.

There's something ironic about our struggles to effect change in organizations. We participate in a world where change is all there is. We sit in the midst of continuous creation, in a universe whose creativity and adaptability are beyond comprehension. Nothing is ever the same twice, really. And in our personal lives, we adapt and change all the time, and we witness this adaptability in our children, friends, colleagues.

It's become common these days to describe organizations as "organic" and "dynamic." But do current practices in organizations resemble those used by life? Do recent organizational change processes feel more alive? *Organic* is a newer buzzword describing the same old organizational processes. These processes remain fundamentally mechanistic. Nowhere is this more apparent than in how we approach organizational change.

Old and New Organizational Change Strategies
Several years ago, we asked a group of engineers and technicians to describe how they went about changing a machine. In neat sequential steps, here's what they described:

1. Assign a manager.
2. Set a goal that is bigger and better.
3. Define the direct outcomes.
4. Determine the measures.
5. Dissect the problem.
6. Redesign the machine.
7. Implement the adaptation.
8. Test the results.
9. Assign blame.

Sound familiar? Doesn't this describe most of the organizational change projects you've been involved in? The one real difference is that most organizations skip step 8. We seldom test the results of our change efforts. We catch a glimmer of the results that are emerging (the unintended consequences) and realize that they're not what we had planned or what we sold to senior leadership. Instead of delving into what the results are—instead of *learning* from this experience— we do everything we can to get attention off the entire project. We spin off into a new project, announce another initiative, reassign managers and teams. Avoiding being the target of blame becomes the central activity rather than learning from what just happened. No wonder we keep failing!

Life changes its forms of organization using an entirely different process. This process can't be described in neat increments or sequential steps. It occurs in the tangled webs of relationships—the networks—that characterize all living systems. There are no simple stages or easy-to-draw causal loops. Changes occur quickly but invisibly, concealed by the density of the network.

If organizations behave like living systems, the following description of change should sound familiar:

Some part of the system (the system can be any size—an organization, a community, a team, a nation) notices something. It might be in a memo, a chance comment, a news report. It chooses to be disturbed by this. *Chooses* is the important word here. No one ever tells a living system what should disturb it (even though we try all the time). If it *chooses* to be disturbed, it takes in the information and circulates it rapidly through its networks. As the disturbance circulates, others grab it and amplify it. The information grows, changes, becomes distorted from the original, but all the time it is accumulating more meaning. Finally, the information becomes so important that the system can't deal with it. Then and only then will the system begin to change. It is forced, by the sheer meaningfulness of the information, to let go of present beliefs, structures, patterns, values. It cannot use its past to make sense of this new information. It truly must let go, plunging itself into a state of confusion and uncertainty that feels like chaos, a state that always feels terrible.

Having fallen apart, having let go of who it has been, the system is now and only now open to change. It will reorganize using new interpretations, new understandings of what's real and what's important. *It becomes different because it understands the world differently.* And, paradoxically, as is true with all living systems, it changed because it was the only way to preserve itself.

If you contemplate the great difference between these two descriptions of change in a machine and in a living system, you may catch a glimpse of what a large task awaits us. We need to better understand the processes by which a living system transforms itself. From that understanding, we will need to rethink how we approach organizational change. We'd like to describe in more detail these processes used by life and their implications for organizational change practices.

Freedom to Create Is Essential for Change

In our lives together, and in our organizations, we must honor the fact that everyone requires the freedom to author their own life. Every person, overtly or covertly, struggles to preserve this freedom to self-create. If you find yourself disagreeing with this statement, think about your experiences with managing others, be they workers, children, or partners. Have you ever had the experience of giving another human being a set of detailed instructions and succeeded in having them follow them exactly? We haven't met anyone who's had this desired experience of complete, robotlike obedience to their directives, so we're assuming that your experience is closer to the following. You give someone clear instructions, written or verbal, and they change it in some way, just a little or a lot. They tweak it, reinterpret it, ignore parts of it, add their own coloration or emphasis. When we see these behaviors, if we're the manager, we feel frustrated or outraged. Why can't they follow directions? Why are they so resistant? Why are they sabotaging my good work?

But there's another interpretation possible, actually inevitable, if we look at this through the lens of living systems. It's not resistance or sabotage or stupidity we're observing. It's the fact that people need to be creatively involved in how their work gets done. We're seeing people exercising their inalienable freedom to create for themselves. They take *our* work and recreate it as *their* work. And this process of re-creation can't be stopped without deadening that person. The price we pay for obedience is that we forfeit vitality and creativity. We submit to another's direction only by playing dead. We end up dispirited, disaffected, and lifeless. And then our superiors wonder why we turned out so badly.

You may think this is an outrageously optimistic view of what's going on in organizations, because undoubtedly you can name those around you who display no creative desires and who only want to be told what to do. But look more closely at their behavior. Is it as robotlike as it first appears? Are they truly passive, or passive-aggressive (just another way some people assert their creativity)? And what are their lives like outside work? How complex is the private life they deal with daily?

Or look at human history. Over and over it testifies to the indomitable human spirit rising up against all forms of oppression. No matter how terrible the oppression, humans find ways to assert themselves. No system of laws or rules can hold us in constraint; no set of directions can tell us exactly how to proceed. We will always bring ourselves into the picture; we will always add our unique signature to the situation. Whether leaders call us innovative or rebellious depends on their comprehension of what's going on.

The inalienable freedom to create one's life shows up in other familiar organizational scenes. People, like the rest of life, maintain the freedom to decide what to notice. We choose what disturbs us. It's not the volume or even the frequency of the message that gets our attention. If it's meaningful to us, we notice it. Most of us have prepared a presentation, a report, a memo about a particular issue because we knew that this issue was critical. Failing to address this would have severe consequences for our group or organization. But when we presented the issue, we were greeted not with enthusiasm and gratitude but with politeness or disinterest. The issue went nowhere. Others dropped it and moved on to what they thought was important. Most often when we have this experience, we interpret their disinterest as our failure to communicate, so we go back and rewrite the report, develop better graphics, create a jazzier presentation style. But none of this matters. Our colleagues are failing to respond because they don't share our sense that this is meaningful. *This is a failure to find shared significance, not a failure to communicate.* They have exercised their freedom and chosen not to be disturbed.

Four Core Principles of Change

If we understand that this essential freedom to create one's self is operating in organizations, we can reinterpret behaviors in a more positive light, and we can begin to think about how to work with this great force (rather than deal with the consequences of ignoring its existence.) Here are four very important principles for practice.

Participation Is Not a Choice
We have no choice but to invite people to rethink, redesign, restructure the organization. We ignore people's need to participate at our own peril. If they're involved, they will create a future that has them in it, that they'll work to make happen. We won't have to engage in the impossible and exhausting tasks of "selling" them the solution, getting them "to enroll," or figuring out the

incentives that might bribe them into compliant behaviors. For the past fifty years, a great bit of wisdom has circulated in the field of organizational behavior: People support what they create. In observing how life organizes, we would restate this maxim as, People *only* support what they create. Life insists on its freedom to participate and can never be coerced into accepting someone else's plans.

After many years of struggling with participative processes, you may hear "participation is not a choice" as no solution at all. But we'd encourage you to think about where your time has gone in change projects. If they were not broadly participative—if they failed to engage all those who had a stake in the issue—how much of your time was spent on managing the unintended effects created by people feeling left out or ignored? How many of your efforts were directed at selling a solution that you knew no one really wanted? How much of your energy went into redesigning the redesign of the redesign after people pointed out its glaring omissions, omissions caused by their lack of involvement in the first redesign?

In our experience, enormous struggles with implementation are created every time we *deliver* changes to the organization rather than figuring out how to involve people in their creation. These struggles are far more draining and prone to failure than what we wrestle with in trying to engage an entire organization. Time and again we've seen implementation move with dramatic speed among people who have been engaged in the design of those changes.

As people are engaged in the difficult and messy processes of participation, they are simultaneously creating the conditions—new relationships, new insights, greater levels of commitment—that facilitate more rapid and complete implementation. But because participative processes can overwhelm us with the complexity of human interactions, many leaders grasp instead for quickly derived solutions from small groups that are then pronounced to the whole organization. Leaders keep hoping this will work—it would make life so much easier! But life won't let it work; people will always resist these impositions. Life, all of life, insists on participation. We can work with this insistence and use it to engage people's creativity and commitment, or we can keep ignoring it and spend most of our time dealing with all the negative consequences.

Life Always Reacts to Directives; It Never Obeys Them
It never matters how clear or visionary or important the message is. It can only elicit reactions, not straightforward compliance. If we recognize that this principle is always at work, it changes expectations of what can be accomplished with any communication. We can expect reactions as varied as the individuals who hear it. If we can offer our work as an invitation to others to engage with us, rather than as a plan or solution, we will develop good, thinking relationships with colleagues. We're inviting them to partner with us. And life accepts only partners, not bosses.

This principle seriously affects leader behaviors. Instead of hunting for the disloyal ones or repeating and repeating the directions, she or he realizes that there is a great deal to be learned from differing reactions. If that diversity is explored, the organization develops a richer, wiser understanding of what's going on. The capacity for learning and growth expands as concerns about loyalty or compliance recede.

As leaders begin to explore the diversity resident in even a small group of people, life asks something else of them. No two reactions will be identical; no two people or events will look the same. Leaders have to forego any desire they have for repetition or sameness, whether it be of persons or processes. Even in industries that are heavily regulated or focused on finely detailed procedures (such as nuclear power plants, hospitals, pharmaceuticals, chemicals), if people only repeat the procedures mindlessly, those procedures eventually fail.

Mistakes and tragedies in these environments bear witness to the effects of lifeless behaviors and indifference bred from repetition.

This is by no means a suggestion to abandon procedures or standardization. But it is crucial to notice that there is no such thing as a humanproof procedure. We have to honor the fact that people always need to include themselves in how a procedure gets done. They accomplish this by understanding the reasoning behind the procedure or by knowing that they are sanctioned to adjust it if circumstances change. We all need to see that there is room for our input, for us, in how our work gets done.

Again, life doesn't give us much choice here. Even if we insist on obedience, we will never gain it for long, and we only gain it at the cost of what we wanted most—loyalty, intelligence and responsiveness.

We Do Not See "Reality"; We Each Create Our Own Interpretation of What's Real
We see the world through who we are, or, as expressed by the poet Michael Chitwood: "What you notice becomes your life." Since no two people are alike, no two people have exactly the same interpretation of what's going on. Yet at work and at home we act as if others see what we see and assign the same meaning as we do to events. We sit in a meeting and watch something happen and just assume that most people in that room, or at least those we trust, saw the same thing. We might even engage them in some quick conver-sation that seems to confirm our sense of unanimity:

  "Did you see what went on in there!?"
  "I know, I couldn't believe what I was seeing."
  "Really!"

But if we stopped to compare further, we'd soon discover significant and useful differences in what we noticed and how we interpreted the situation.

It's not about arguing about who's right and who's wrong. If we talk with colleagues to share perceptions, if we expect and even seek out the great diversity of interpretations that exist, we learn and change. Biologist Francisco Varela redefined organizational intelligence: It isn't the ability to solve problems that makes an organization smart. It is the ability of its members to enter into a world whose significance they share. Everyone in the group has to feel that what is occurring is significant—even as they have different perspectives.

Entering into a world of shared significance is only achieved by engaging in conversations with colleagues. Not debates or oratories, but conversation that welcomes in the unique perspective of everyone there. If we remain *curious* about what someone else sees and refrain from convincing them of our interpretation, we develop a richer view of what might be going on. And we also create collegial relations that enable us to work together with greater speed and effectiveness. When any of us feel invited to share our perspective, we repay that respect and trust with commitment and friendship.

A very important paradox becomes evident. We don't have to agree on an interpretation or hold identical values in order to agree on what needs to be done. We don't have to settle for the lowest common denominator, or waste hours and hours politicking for our own, decided-on-ahead-of-time solution. As we sit together and listen to so many differing perspectives, we get off our soapboxes and open to new ways of thinking. We have allowed these new perspectives to disturb us, and we've changed. And surprisingly, this enables us to agree on a concerted course of action and to support it wholeheartedly. This paradox flies in the face of how we've tried to reach group consensus, but it makes good sense from a living system's perspective. We all need to participate, and when we're offered that opportunity, we then want to work with others. We've entered into a world whose significance is shared by all of us, and because of that process we've developed a lot of energy for deciding *together* what to do next.

To Create Better Health in a Living System, Connect It to More of Itself

When a system is failing, or performing poorly, the solution will be discovered *within the system* if more and better connections are created. The solution is always to bring the system together so that it can learn more about itself from itself. A troubled system needs to start talking to itself, especially to those it didn't know were even part of itself. The value of this practice was quite evident at the beginning of the customer service revolution, when talking to customers and dealing with the information they offered became a potent method for stimulating the organization to new levels of quality. Without customer feedback, workers couldn't know what or how to change. Quality standards rose dramatically once customers were connected to the system.

This principle embodies a profound respect for systems. It says that they are capable of changing themselves, once they are provided with new and richer information. It says that they have a natural tendency to move toward better functioning or health. It assumes that the system already has within it most of the expertise that it needs. This principle also implies that the critical task for a leader is to increase the number, variety and strength of connections within the system. Bringing in remote or ignored members, providing access across the system, and through those connections stimulating the creation of new information—all of these become primary tasks for fostering organizational change. These four principles provide very clear indicators of how, within our organizations, we can work with life's natural tendency to learn and change. As we all were taught by an advertisement many years ago, we can't fool Mother Nature. If we insist on developing organizational change processes suited for machines and ignore life's need to participate in things that concern it, then we can only anticipate more frequent and costly failures.

Principles, Not Techniques

The organization found in living systems is always highly complex. But this complexity is obtained by an organizing process that is simple and that honors the individual's need to participate. The complexity is the result of individuals interpreting, in the moment, a few simple principles. These simple principles are not negotiable and cannot be ignored. But how they get interpreted depends on the immediate circumstance and the individuals involved at that time. Everyone is accountable to the principles, yet everyone is free to figure out how to apply them. This process of organizing honors individual freedom, engages creativity and individuality, yet simultaneously achieves an orderly and coherent organization.

From such simple agreements complex organizations arise. Structures, norms, networks of communication develop from the constant interactions among system members as they interpret the principles in different circumstances. Sophisticated organizational forms appear, but always these materialize from the inside out. They are never imposed from the outside in.

We humans have spent so many years determining the details of the organization—its structures, values, communication channels, vision, standards, measures. Living systems have all these features and details, but they originate differently. As we think of organizations as living systems, we don't discard our concern for such things as standards, measures, values, organizational structures, plans. We don't give up any of these. But we do need to change our beliefs about where these things come from. In a living system, they are generated as people figure out what will work well in the current situation. In a machine these features are designed outside and then engineered in.

We can easily discern whether we are approaching organizations as a living system or as a machine by asking, Who created any aspect of the organization? We know we need structure, plans, measures, but who gets to create them? The source of authorship makes all the difference.

The junior high school principal who created a complex and orderly system from a few simple principles is worth looking at again. Most school administrators fear adolescents and the typical junior high school has unending rules and procedures to police the hormone-crazed tendencies of early teens. But this junior high school of eight hundred students successfully operated from three rules. Everyone—students, teachers, staff—knew the rules and used them to deal with all situations. While disarmingly simple, these three were all that were needed: (1) Take care of yourself; (2) take care of each other; (3) take care of this place. Few of us would believe that you could create an orderly group of adolescents, let alone a good learning environment, from such simple rules.

Simple rules define what we have decided is significant to us as a community or organization. They contain our agreements about what we will pay attention to, what we will let disturb us. In the case of these students, when they returned to the school after being evacuated for a fire, wet shoes and muddy floors were something they quickly noticed, because they had already agreed to "take care of this place." When they returned and took their shoes off in the lobby, they were creating a specific response to that general rule.

Using Principles Rather Than Models

In deciding on what to emphasize in this essay, we knew that you required even more freedom than these students to design organizational change processes that would work best in your unique situation. Therefore, we chose to give you principles to work with, principles that evoke life's capacity for change. As with all principles, once they are agreed upon, they need to be taken very seriously. They are the standards to which we hold ourselves accountable. But clear principles provide only standards; they never describe the details of how to do something. They do not restrict our creativity; they simply guide our designs and create coherence among our many diverse efforts. Their clarity serves as an invitation to be creative. Think about how many *different* approaches and techniques you could create that would be congruent with the four principles stated here. How many different forms of practice could materialize as people in your organization invented change processes that honored these principles?

No two change processes need look the same. In fact this is an impossibility— no technique ever materializes in the same way twice. Nothing transfers unchanged. (If it did, no one would be struggling with the issue of organizational change. We'd have found what worked somewhere else and successfully imported it.) But if we hold ourselves accountable to these principles, we can create our own unique change processes, confident that we are working *with* life rather than denying it. We will have been guided by these principles to create processes that take advantage of the creativity and desire to contribute that reside in the vast majority of the people in our organizations.

Conduct Experiments

We'd like to invite you to experiment with this approach and these four principles. As with all good experiments, this means that you try something new, and then you watch what happens and learn from the results. Good experimentation is a process, making little adjustments as the results come in, trying to discover what's responsible for the effects that show up. So for whatever you start in motion, it's essential to watch it carefully as it unfolds, involving many eyes in the observing.

You might experiment with these four principles in a project design team, either one that's just starting or one that's trying to rescue a change process that's not working well. See what actions and strategies can be created as you hold your- selves accountable to these principles. Think through the implications of these principles with others in the organization. Experiment with a design that feels congruent with the principles, and once that design is operating, observe carefully where it needs to be modified or changed. Stay with it as an experiment rather than as the solution.

A second experiment can occur in every meeting, task force, or event in your organization. This experiment requires the discipline to ask questions. Each question opens up an inquiry. The questions keep people focused on critical issues. Here are four possible questions to consider asking:

1. Who else needs to be here?
2. What just happened?
3. Can we talk?
4. Who have we become?

The simplicity of these questions may lead you to believe they're not sufficient or important, but think about the types of inquiry they invite. Every time we ask, "Who else needs to be here?" we're called to notice the system of relationships that is pertinent to the issue at hand. We're willing to be alert to who's missing, and the earlier we notice who's missing, the sooner we can include them. This question helps us move to broader participation gradually and thoughtfully, as the result of what we're learning about the issue and the organization. It's an extremely simple but powerful method for becoming good systems thinkers and organizers.

Similarly, "What just happened?" is a question that leads to learning from our experience. Since living systems always react but never obey, this question focuses us on what we might learn if we look at the reactions that just surfaced. The question moves us away from blame and instead opens us to learning a great deal about who this system is and what grabs its attention.

When we ask, "Can we talk?" we're acknowledging that others perceive the world differently from us. Imagine leaving a typical meeting where ego battles predominated. Instead of posturing, grumbling, or politicking, what if we went up to those we disagreed with and asked to talk with them. What if we were sincerely interested in trying to see the world from their perspective? Would this enable us to work together more effectively?

"Who have we become?" is a query that keeps us noticing how we are creating ourselves—not through words and position papers, but through our actions and reactions from moment to moment. All living systems spin themselves into existence because of what they choose to notice and how they choose to respond. This is also true of human organizations, so we need to acknowledge that we are constantly creating the organization through our responses. To monitor our own evolution, we need to ask this question regularly. Without such monitoring, we may be shocked to realize who we've become while we weren't watching. And for organizations that put in place a few essential rules, like that junior high school, everyone periodically needs to review how they're doing. Are the core principles discernible in our actions? Are they creating the organization that people envisioned?

Questions require discipline in asking them, a discipline we seldom practice. No matter how simple the questions, we most often rush past them. We feel compelled to act rather than to inquire. But by now, many of us in organizations want to turn away from this history of act! act! act! that leads to no learning and so much wasted energy. All other forms of life stay constantly alert and responsive—they learn continuously, as science writer James Gleick notes: "Life learned itself into existence." Physicist and author Fritjof Capra often states that there is no distinction between living and learning, "A living system is a learning system." If we don't begin to seriously focus on learning in our organizations, there is no way we can bring them to life.

Throughout this essay, we've stressed the freedom to create that all life requires. We hope that you will feel inspired to exercise your freedom and creativity to experiment with some of the ideas, principles, and questions we've noted. We need each other's best thinking and most courageous experiments if we are to create a future worth wanting.

Working with Life's Dynamics in School Systems

People speak so easily these days of systems—systems thinking, systems change, connectivity, networks. Yet in my experience, we really don't know what these terms mean or their implications for our work. We don't yet know how to act in or think about this new interconnected world of systems that we've created.

Those of us educated in Western culture learned to think and manage a world that was anything but systemic or interconnected. It's a world of separations and clear boundaries: jobs in boxes, lines delineating relationships, roles and policies describing what each individual does and who we expect them to be. Western culture is very skilled at describing the world by these strange, unnatural separations.

We also have believed that, by using these approaches, we could control everything. From manipulating the weather, to stopping aging and death, we hope that science will eventually give us complete power over life. At the organizational level, we strive for a similar level of control. We want to be able to make people, communities, and entire organizations act according to *our* plans and directives. We want strong, take-charge leaders who know exactly what's going on, have all the answers, and inspire us with their vision.

By now, most of us have been in organizations and lives that have revealed to us the foolishness of these assumptions. No matter how well we plan, how carefully we analyze a situation, or how strong a leader we find, we don't succeed nearly as often as we need to. We put more and more effort into planning and leadership approaches that seem only to lead us ever farther away from our goals and aspirations. We have suffered from the unending fads that, like great tidal waves, crash down on our schools, creating more destruction than growth. As the most recent wave recedes, we look over our schools and see debris scattered everywhere—relationships torn apart, survivors struggling to come up for air, ideas and plans tossed askew.

In corporations, fads have failed in exactly the same manner, creating great wreckage. Corporations are no better than any other sector at knowing how to create needed changes, even though school leaders still look to them for the next new idea. It usually shocks those in education to hear that not only schools are failing miserably, but so is every major institutional form, whether public or private, for profit or for public benefit. Corporate CEOs report a startling record of failures of their major change initiatives—up to 75 percent. How many in education would garner support for a project that was successful only 25 percent of the time?

We Need a New Worldview

Nothing today is simple or slow. This means we can't make sense of the world using the analytical processes we were taught or understand the complexity of modern systems by reductionism. In a complex system, it is impossible to find simple causes that explain our problems or to know who to blame. A messy tangle of relationships is responsible for these unending crises. We need a different way to understand and work in this new world of continuous change and intimately connected systems that reach around the globe.

Again, we turn to life to learn how complex systems change, flex, and grow. For four to five billion years, life has been developing its infinite variety, surprising scientists by showing up in the coldest and hottest habitats, places where science thought no life could ever exist. Life is a rich source of ideas and wisdom for how we can approach the challenge of creating schools that have the capacity to change successfully.

A primary lesson of life is that nothing living lives alone. Life always and only organizes as systems of interdependency. Until the advent of Western ideas in the seventeenth century, most humans and spiritual traditions described life in terms of this interdependency and connectedness. But the machine imagery that underpins modern society dismisses this. It replaces dense webs of connections with predesigned charts and plans that describe who is connected to whom. There's no recognition that life knows how to organize itself. We replaced life's capacity for self-organization with the belief that without human organizing skills, nothing gets done. If we don't take control, there is only chaos. We don't seem to notice how our attempts *to impose order* create just the opposite effect, *more disorder*.

By now, we've lost sight of the many processes by which life gives birth to order. In our blindness, we struggle with processes that fail to work *with* life, that in fact are antithetical to how life works. The result is the sorry chronicle of failure at organizational change. It is time to wake up to the fact that we live in an interconnected world, embedded in a fabric of relationships that requires us to pay attention to the dynamics of systems, not to isolated individuals or events.

Life's Dynamics for Self-Organization and Change
I'd like to share a few of the dynamics that operate in every living system, and then describe ways to work with them in organizational change efforts.

A Living System Forms from Shared Interests
Although systems are naturally occurring, they do not form at random. A living system is created as individuals notice they have shared interests. Individuals realize that they have neighbors and that they would do better to figure out how to live together than to try and destroy each other. The recognition that individuals need each other lies at the heart of every system. From that realization, individuals reach out, and seemingly divergent self-interests develop into a

system of interdependency. Thus, all systems form through collaboration, from the recognition that we need another in order to survive.

We humans have a great need for relationships and meaningful lives. We seek to connect with those whose self-interest seems to include or impact our own interests. We affiliate with those who share a similar sense of what is important. When you apply this dynamic to public education, it instantly reveals a major dilemma. *Is a school system really a system?* Human systems never form just as a result of geography, so it isn't district lines drawn on paper that create a school system. Systems take form because people realize that in order to achieve what is important to them, they must extend themselves and work with others.

How many members of a geographically determined school district share the same beliefs about the purpose of education? Most districts contain a wide spectrum of beliefs about the role of education. There are those who believe that education should support the talented elite, which includes their child. Those who view education as the foundation of a pluralistic society where education should open doors for all. Those who believe in a rich life of the mind. Those who want their children trained for immediate employment. Those who want their children taught only the values of their parents or church.

The startling conclusion is that most school systems aren't systems. They are only boundary lines drawn by somebody, somewhere. They are not systems because they do not arise from a core of shared beliefs about the purpose of public education. In the absence of shared beliefs and desires, people are not motivated to seek out one another and develop relationships. Instead, they inhabit the same organizational and community space without weaving together mutually sustaining relationships. They coexist by defining clear boundaries, creating respectful and disrespectful distances, developing self-protective behaviors, and using power politics to get what they want.

Yet everyone who participates in a school district *is* a living being, responding to the same dynamics that characterize all other life. Within the artificial boundary lines and well-defended territories, people are self-organizing into real systems, reaching out to network with those who share similar beliefs or aspirations. (This dynamic is clearly evident in the charter school movement.) Many small systems are created within the artificial system of a district. It is these real systems that become clearly visible when we try to change the artificial ones. People often startle us with the ferocity with which they confront and impede our efforts. But it is these real systems we must work with if we want to effect change.

All Change Results from a Change in Meaning
People, like all forms of life, only change when something so disturbs them that they are forced to let go of their present beliefs. Nothing changes until we interpret things differently. Change occurs only when we let go of our certainty, our current views, and develop a new understanding of what's going on.

See if the following process of change—how life changes—feels accurate to you. Someone in the school or community get upset by something. He or she communicates their upset, and it circulates through the network. Once inside the web of relationships, a small disturbance grows and morphs as it is passes from person to person. It gets quite distorted from the original information, but, as it circulates, it grows in meaning. Finally, the whole system sits up and takes notice.

We've all had this experience, probably many times. A casual or offhand comment tossed out in a meeting gets picked up by someone in the organization, and suddenly we're in the midst of a firestorm of opinions, emotions, and rumors. Or something distressing happens in a school, such as a violent incident, and everyone realizes that things are not as they seemed.

At this point, when the disturbance is at its greatest, change is at hand. The system has been knocked completely off-balance; it can't make sense of the information by relying on past practice or beliefs. The system is forced to abandon its current construct of the world. It *unwillingly* plunges into confusion and uncertainty. But now that it has fallen apart, real change is possible. It will change because it sees the world differently. It will reorganize using new interpretations, new meaning. For change to occur, there must be a change in meaning.

Every Living System Is Free to Choose Whether It Changes
We never succeed in directing or telling people how they must change. We don't succeed by handing them a plan, or pestering them with our interpretations, or relentlessly pressing forward with our agenda, believing that volume and intensity will convince them to see it our way. You can scream and holler as much as you want, but if people don't regard what you're saying as important, they'll just ignore you and go on with their own life. (In this way, all people behave like teenagers.)

It is impossible to impose anything on people. We must participate in anything that affects us. We can't act on behalf of anyone, we can't figure out what's best for somebody else. If leaders or task forces refuse to believe this and go ahead and make plans for us, we don't sit by passively and do what we're told. We still get involved, but from the sidelines, where we've been told to sit and wait. We get involved by ignoring, resisting, or sabotaging all plans and directives that are imposed on us.

One school superintendent reported wryly how he learned that his committee approach to curriculum development wasn't working. Every summer, he would appoint a group of four or five teachers from each discipline to develop materials for the coming year. He was pleased with their products and often commented on their creativity. Sometime during the late autumn, as the super-intendent made site visits, he would ask teachers how they liked the new materials. It took him too many years, he said, to realize that the only teachers using the materials were those members of the committee that had created them.

This is not an unusual experience for any of us. How many strategic plans, policy manuals, and curriculum materials collect dust on our shelves because we were not involved in their creation? Confronted by so much evidence, we could have learned long ago that people must always participate in the development of those things which affect them.

Systems Contain Their Own Solutions
Living systems contain their own solutions. Somewhere in the system are people already practicing a solution that others think is impossible. Or they possess information that could help many others. Or, they defy stereotypes and have the very capabilities we need.

To find these solutions, the system needs to connect to more of itself. This means meeting with those we've excluded or avoided, those we never imagined could share similar interests. Deep inside a school, we often forget how many others—parents, community employers, public officials—care about what's going on in the classroom. When we invite these people in from the periphery, when we find ways to sit and listen to them, it is a wonderful surprise to discover our connections. We realize that we have common aspirations for our children, that we share many things in common despite our many differences.

It is crucial to remember that, in organizations, we are working with webs of relationships. As webs, there is a lot to be learned about organizational change from contemplating spider webs. Most of us have had the experience of touching a spider web, feeling its resiliency, noticing how slight pressure in one area jiggles the entire web. If a web breaks and needs repair, the spider doesn't cut out a piece, terminate it, or tear the entire web apart and reorganize it. She reweaves it, using the silken relationships that are already there, creating stronger connections across the weakened spaces.

At this time in our history, we are in great need of processes that can help us weave ourselves back together. We've lost confidence in our great human capabilities, partly because mechanistic organizational processes have separated and divided us, and made us fearful and distrusting of one another. We need processes to help us reweave connections, to discover shared interests, to listen to one another's stories and dreams. We need processes that take advantage of our natural ability to network, to communicate when something is meaningful to us. We need processes that invite us to participate, that honor our creativity and commitment to the organization.

Life's Dynamics for Self-organization and Change
- *A living system forms from shared interests.*
- *All change results from a change in meaning.*
- *Every living system is free to choose whether it changes.*
- *Systems contain their own solutions.*

Working with Life's Dynamics to Create Change

If our intent is to help a school system change, we need to take these four dynamics seriously. Most change efforts (in all types of organizations) ignore every one of them. The result is not only failure to change but exhaustion and cynicism. How much time and resources have been wasted trying to force schools and people to change according to an imposed plan and process.

I'd like to describe how working with these dynamics can dramatically change our approaches and our success with organizational change.

Discover What's Meaningful

Both individual and organizational change start from the same need: the need to discover what's meaningful. People change *only* if they believe that a new insight, a new idea, or a new form is important to them. If it is a larger unit, such as a school or community, the search for new meaning must occur as a collective activity. People need to discover that there is sufficient shared interest among the community, shared meaning strong enough to bring people together and to hold them together as they do the work.

Discover One Another

Discovering shared interests, even small ones, changes people's relationships for the better. If we recognize a shared sense of injustice or a shared dream, magical things happen to our relationships; we open to each other as colleagues. Past hurts and negative histories get left behind. People step forward to work together. We don't hang back; we don't withdraw; we don't wait to be enticed. We seek each other out, eager to discover others who might help. The call of meaning, the importance of the problem, sounds louder than past grievances or our fears that we don't know how to have an impact. *If we can discover something important to work on together, we figure out how to do the work, together.*

I've worked with a number of faculties torn apart by the impact of technology. The more technologically eager faculty accuse the reticent ones of being out-of-date and resistant to change—they berate their colleagues for not climbing on the technology bandwagon. I always suggest that a different conversation is needed. What if we stop assuming that technology's value to a teacher is self-evident? What if we stop assuming that anybody who doesn't adopt new technology is an antiquated Luddite whose only interest is to stop the march of progress? If we give up those assumptions, we can begin a different conversation, one that helps us connect to one another and learn more about what we each find meaningful in our profession. *We need to step back from the technology issue and ask one another what called us into teaching.* We listen to the aspirations that are voiced. And what we always hear is that most of us went into teaching for noble purposes—we wanted to make a difference in the lives of young people; we were excited to help kids learn.

If we have this conversation first, we discover one another as colleagues. We realize we want very similar things. We realize that the person we had judged as dead on the job still carries a passion for learning. Or that the teacher who belittles students still cares about them. Now we can talk about technology. How might computers assist colleagues to become more effective at their craft? How might technology make it easier to do the work they have defined as meaningful? If those links are made, *then* colleagues log on to e-mail and use the computers sitting on their desks to enhance student learning. And if they don't, at least we know them now as colleagues, not problems.

This process of inquiring together about the meaning of our work also helps us stop the labeling behavior that is far too prevalent these days. We are quick to assign colleagues and students to a typology or a syndrome, and then dismiss them, as if this tells us enough about them. There have been more than enough studies in education that prove how teacher perceptions influence student behaviors. It would be good for us to learn from these, and free ourselves from all this labeling that creates such negative consequences.

Use the Network's Communication Capacity

Living networks display incredible communicating power when information is meaningful to them. Meaningful information lights up a network and moves through it like a windswept brush fire. Meaningless information, in contrast, smolders at the gates until somebody dumps cold water on it. The capacity of a network to communicate with itself is truly awe-inspiring; its transmission capability far surpasses any other mode of communication. But a living network will only transmit what it decides is meaningful. I have watched information move instantaneously across great distances in a global company; I have watched information in four-color graphics die before it ever came off the printer. To use a network's communication capacity, we must notice that its transmission power is directly linked to the meaningfulness of the information.

Meaning behaves like energy. It doesn't behave in mechanistic ways. Therefore, we can abandon many of our mechanistic assumptions about what is required for organizational change. We don't have to achieve "critical mass"; we don't need programs that "roll out" (or over) the entire organization; we don't need to train every individual or part; we can stop obsessing if we don't get the support of the top of the organization. Instead, we can work locally, finding the ideas and processes that are meaningful in one area of the system. If we succeed in generating energy in one area, we can watch how our other networks choose to notice what we're doing. Who takes notice? Where have our ideas traveled in the organizational web? If we ask these questions, we learn who might be ready to take up this work next. My colleague Myron Rogers describes this approach to organizational change as "Start anywhere and follow it everywhere."

Involve Everybody Who Cares

For too many years, I've learned the hard way that participation is the only change process. Any time I've used only a small group, nothing has worked well. As organizational change facilitators and leaders, we must invite in all those who will be affected by the change. Those whom we fail to invite into the change process are the very people who will poison our process. But broad-based participation is not just a strategy to avoid resistance or to find supporters. The simple fact is that we can't design anything that works without the involvement of all those it affects. None of us is smart enough these days to know what will work for others. We can't see what's meaningful to them, and we're ignorant about their work situation. The complexity of systems requires that we engage everybody just so we can harvest the intelligence that exists throughout the organization.

There is a great deal of evidence for how well whole systems change processes work. What is lacking are not case examples or processes but the commitment to involve everybody. We keep hoping we don't need to—that if we design a good plan, people will accept it on its merits. We haven't yet absorbed the simple truth that we can't force anybody to change. We can only involve them in the change process from the beginning and see what's possible. If change becomes meaningful to them, they will change. If we want their support, we must welcome them as cocreators.

Learn as You Go

Shifting our approaches to organizational change, so that we are working *with* life's change dynamics, is a gradual process that requires patience, generosity, and time. No one is able to act in new ways just because they decide to. We all get yanked back to old ways of doing things, especially when we feel tense or confused. All groups need to keep alert to their process, their learnings, and how the change effort is unfolding and emerging. This watchfulness is accomplished simply by developing a set of questions that the group commits to asking regularly, and with discipline. Here are some examples of the types of questions that work, but it's important to create your own and then hold yourself responsible for asking them frequently:

Key Questions to Keep Asking
- *Who's missing? Who else needs to do this work?*
- *Is the meaning of this work still clear? Is it changing?*
- *Are we becoming more truthful with each other?*
- *Is information becoming more open and easier to access?*
- *Where are we using imposition? Participation?*
- *What are we learning about partnering with confusion and chaos?*

Trusting That Life Can Organize Itself

I have to admit that the greatest challenge for me and those I work with lies not in adopting new methods but in learning to live in this process world. It's a completely new way to be, unlike anything I was taught. I'm learning to participate with things as they unfold, to expect to be surprised, to enjoy the mystery of it, and to surrender to what I don't know and can never know. These were difficult lessons to learn. I was well trained to create things—plans, policies, events, programs. I invested more than half my life in trying to make the world conform to what I thought was best. It hasn't been easy to give up the role of master creator and move into the dance of life.

But I've gradually learned there is no alternative. As our dance partner, life insists that we put ourselves in motion, that we learn to live with instability, chaos, change, and surprise. We can continue to stand immobilized on the shoreline, trying to protect ourselves from life's insistent storms, or we can begin moving. We can watch our plans be washed away, or we can discover something new.

Being present for what's happening in the moment doesn't mean that we act without intention or flow directionless through life without a plan. But in an unpredictable world, we would do better to look at plans and measures as *processes* that enable a group to discover shared interests, to clarify its intent and strengthen its connections to new people and new information. We need less reverence for the plan as an object and much more attention to the processes we use for planning and measuring. It is attention to the process, more than the product, that enables us to weave an organization as flexible and resilient as a spider's web.

As we learn to live and work in this process world, we are rewarded with other changes in our behavior. We become gentler people. We become more curious about differences, more respectful of one another, more open to life's surprises. Although life's dance can look chaotic from the outside, difficult to learn and impossible to master, our newfound gentleness speaks to a different learning. Life is a good partner. Its demands are not unreasonable. A great capacity for change lives in everyone of us.

When Change Is Out of Our Control

In June 2002, the chief financial officer of Oracle Corporation spoke on prospects for the second half of the year (as reported in the Wall Street Journal). His comments were radically different from the upbeat statements typical of one in his position: "We are hoping for a revenue recovery in the second half of the year. But I said that same thing six months ago, and I have lost confidence in my ability to predict the future."

In his humility, this CFO described the new world of the twenty-first century—this interconnected planet of increased uncertainty and volatility. Organizations are now confronted with two sources of change: the traditional type that is initiated and managed, and external changes over which no one has control. We are just beginning to experience what it is like to operate in a global environment of increasing chaos, of events beyond our control that have a devastating impact on our internal operations and culture.

The business news is filled with stories of the perils of interconnectedness. One country suffers economic problems, and analysts are quick to say that their problems will not affect other countries. Then we watch as an entire continent and those beyond are pulled into economic recession by the web of interdependence. Or we read how the actions of a few corrupt executives bring down an entire company (and industry), even though tens of thousands of people work there with integrity.

Interconnected systems are always this sensitive. Activities occurring in one part of the system always affect many other parts of the system. The nature of the global business environment guarantees that no matter how hard we work to create a stable and healthy organization, our organization will continue to experience dramatic changes far beyond our control. For example, Continental Airlines had spent years developing a strong culture. "Our employees believe in this company and will do anything for our president." (All quotes in this article, unless otherwise noted, are from personal interviews conducted in July 2002 by the author.) But then came September 11, and Continental, like all airlines, suddenly found its entire industry and business model at risk.

No company, industry, or nation is immune to these potentially devastating system effects. One executive in a large corporation commented, "It was always dysfunctional, but it was working. Now it's not. It's a different feeling than years ago. Now we can't influence outcomes. We're 'at the top' but feeling that things are being 'done to' us." Another executive said simply, "What used to work, doesn't. The old strategies don't work."

When so much is beyond our control, when senior leaders reveal their own feelings of powerlessness, what skills can we call upon to successfully maneuver and survive the turbulence?

New Organizational Dynamics

In an era of increasing uncertainty, new organizational dynamics appear, and old ones intensify at all levels of the organization. It is important to notice how these dynamics affect employees, leaders, and core operating functions.

Employee Behaviors

Uncertainty leads to increased fear. As fear levels rise, it is normal for people to focus on personal security and safety. We tend to withdraw, become more self-serving and more defensive. We focus on smaller and smaller details, those things we *can* control. It becomes more difficult to work together and nearly impossible to focus on the bigger picture. And there are physiological impacts as well. Stress deprives the human brain of its ability to see patterns. People become reactive and lose the capacity to understand their work as part of a larger system. We also have difficulty with memory and become forgetful. And then there are the physical manifestations of sleeplessness, restlessness, sudden anger, and unpredictable tears.

Obviously, each of these has negative consequences on work behaviors for individuals and teams. As people experience their growing incapacity to get work done well, they often blame themselves for failing to produce. One woman executive expressed, "So many good people are failing at the changes they're committed to."

Pressures on Leaders

Because of increased fear, many people turn to leaders with unreasonable demands. We want someone to rescue us, to save us, to provide answers, to give us firm ground or strong life rafts. We push for a strong leader to get us out of this mess, even if it means surrendering individual freedom to gain security. But the causes of insecurity are complex and systemic. There is no one simple answer, and not even the strongest of leaders can deliver on the promise of stability and security. We seldom acknowledge that. Instead, we fire the leader and continue searching for the perfect one. A troubled male executive described it this way: "We still charge the leader to provide solutions. When he doesn't, we then sacrifice the king/priest to atone for the sins of the system."

It is critical that leaders resist assuming the role of savior, even as people beg for it. This can be extremely difficult as people grow more fearful and fragile. Sophisticated emotional skills are required, especially if people have been directly affected by external events. In these cases, the leader must simultaneously struggle to provide emotional support while also working to maintain decent levels of productivity. If the leader has also been personally affected by recent organizational challenges, it becomes very difficult to inspire confidence. As one woman leader asked: "How do you maintain credibility when you (as the leader) are not sure you want to be there?"

Rethinking Core Business Functions

It wasn't long ago that companies engaged in five-year strategic planning. Those sweet, slow days seem very distant now. Many of the primary functions of business—planning, forecasting, budgeting, staffing, development—only worked because we could bring the future into focus, because the future felt within our control. Shortly after September 11, the CEO of a major technology company reported that it was impossible to do a reliable budget for the coming year, even though they had a very good record at budget forecasting in the past. His proposed solution for dealing with so much uncertainty was to submit five alternative budget scenarios to his board.

It is important to note how many people in organizations have honed their skills at predicting or anticipating the future. Businesses have depended on and rewarded their expertise. But now these skills can be a liability. They may lull the organization into a false sense of security about a predictable future and thereby keep people from staying alert to what's going on around them in the present. Yet even though they may be a liability, often such experts are charged with bringing stability back to the organization. The organization may clamor for new planning tools and processes, and push hard on planning staff to find new modes of prediction. Such staff often suffer severe burnout as they work zealously on the impossible task of stabilizing an inherently temperamental world. A wise planning executive commented on how he has changed expectations of his function: "I tell people we're not going to get any more clarity. This is as good as it gets."

The Great Paradox

I have painted a fairly grim picture of these new organizational dynamics spawned by tumultuous times. However, there is a great paradox that points to the hopeful path ahead: *It is possible to prepare for the future without knowing what it will be.* The primary way to prepare for the unknown is to attend to the quality of our relationships, to how well we know and trust one another. In New York City and Oklahoma City, as well as many other disaster situations, people had engaged in emergency preparedness drills prior to having to deal with the real thing. Working together on these simulations, they developed cohesive, trusting relationships and interagency cooperation. They had only prepared for simpler disasters, but when terror struck, they knew they could rely on each other. Elizabeth Dole, when president of the American Red Cross, said that she didn't wait until the river was flooding at two in the morning to pick up the phone and establish a relationship.

When people know they can rely on each other, when there is a true sense of community, it is amazing how well people perform. This was the experience of the community of Halifax, Nova Scotia, on September 11. Forty-two planes were grounded at their small airport, and eight thousand distressed and stranded passengers suddenly appeared on their doorstep. The community's open-hearted response transformed the city and led to relationships with strangers that will last a lifetime. As one community person described it: "It was one of those times when nothing was planned, but everything went so smoothly. Everybody just kind of pulled together."

New Organizational Capabilities

In order to counter the negative organizational dynamics stimulated by stress and uncertainty, we must give full attention to the quality of our relationships. Nothing else works, no new tools or technical applications, no redesigned organizational chart. *The solution is each other.* If we can rely on one another, we can cope with almost anything. Without each other, we retreat into fear.

There is one core principle for developing these relationships. People must be engaged in meaningful work together if they are to transcend individual concerns and develop new capacities. Here are several ways to put this principle into practices.

Nourish a Clear Organizational Identity

As confusion and fear swirls about the organization, people find stability and security in purpose, not in plans. Organizational identity describes who we are, the enduring values we work from, the shared aspirations of who we want to be in and for the world. When chaos wipes the ground from beneath us, the organization's identity gives us some place to stand. When the situation grows confusing, our values provide the means to make clear and good decisions. A clear sense of organizational (and personal) identity gives people the capacity to respond intelligently in the moment, and to choose actions that are congruent. Times of crisis always display the coherence or incoherence at the heart of our organization. Are we pulling together or rushing off in many different directions? Are people's actions and choices congruent with the stated values, or are they basing their decisions on different values. If they are using different values, are these the real rules of the game, the true although unspoken values?

It is crucial to keep organizational purpose and values in the spotlight. The values come to life not through speeches and plaques, but as we hear the stories of other employees who embody those values. It is important to use all existing communication tools, and invent new ones, to highlight these personal experiences. In the year following September 11, United Airlines (whose plane crashed into the Twin Towers), communicated this type of story twice weekly as one means to support employees during very difficult times.

Focus People on the Bigger Picture
People who are stressed lose the ability to recognize patterns, to see the bigger picture. And as people become overloaded and overwhelmed with their tasks, they have no time or interest to look beyond the demands of the moment. Therefore, it is essential that the organization sponsor processes that bring people together so that they can learn of one another's perspectives and challenges. If the organization doesn't make these processes happen, people will continue to spiral inward. This inward spiraling has a devastating impact on performance. People become overwhelmed by the volume of tasks, they lose all sense of meaning for their work, and they feel increasingly isolated and alone. Everybody is busier and more frantic, but the major thing they produce is more

stress. The other serious consequence is that both individual and organizational intelligence decline dramatically as people lose the larger context of their work.

It is important that the processes used for bringing people together not be formal. People need less formality and more conviviality. They need time to decompress and to relax enough to be able to listen to one another. Processes, such as conversation and storytelling, help us connect at a depth not available through charts and PowerPoint presentations. However, people don't recognize how much they need this time, and usually resist such informal gatherings—until they attend one and notice what they've been missing.

Communicate Honestly and Quickly

In a disaster or crisis, the continuous flow of information gives people the capacity to respond intelligently as they seek to rescue and save people and property. They are hungry for information so that they can respond well to urgent human needs. They take in the information, make fast judgment calls, try something, quickly reject it if it doesn't work, and then try something else. They call to one another, exchanging information and learnings. They contribute what they can to everyone becoming more effective in the rescue effort.

Even though most organizations don't deal with this level of crisis, the lessons are important. People deal far better with uncertainty and stress when they know what's going on, even if the information is incomplete and only temporarily correct. Freely circulating information helps create trust, and it turns us into rapid learners and more effective workers. Often, it is not the actual situation that induces stress as much as it is that people aren't told what's going on, or feel deceived. The greater the crisis, the more we need to know. The more affected we are by the situation, the more information we need.

We can observe this need after every commercial air crash when the families who have lost loved ones complain about not being adequately informed by the airlines. They want to know details of how their loved one died, a disclosure that often brings relief to those grieving. Yet the airlines are constrained by potential legal liability from sharing the details that would ease their grief. The families end up suing the airline to get the information, adding emotional damages to their suit. This devastating cycle is fed by feelings of rage and loss that are exacerbated by lack of information.

Prepare for the Unknown

The U.S. military has invested large sums of money in the development and use of complex simulations that prepare troops for different battle scenarios. Similar simulations now are used by most civil defense and community agencies. Yet it is surprising how few companies engage in any type of simulation or scenario work. The evidence is dramatically clear that this type of preparation allows people to move into the unknown with greater skillfulness and capacity. While traditional planning processes no longer work, it is dangerous to abandon thinking about the future. We need to explore these newer methods that project us into *alternative* futures. As people engage in processes such as scenario building or disaster simulations, they feel more capable to deal with uncertainty. Individual and collective intelligence increase dramatically, as people become better-informed big-picture thinkers. And trusting relationships develop that make it possible to call on one another when chaos strikes.

Keep Meaning at the Forefront

Often in organizations we forget that meaning is the most powerful motivator of human behavior. People gain energy and resolve if they understand how their work contributes to something beyond themselves. When we are frightened, we may first focus on our own survival, but we're capable of more generous and altruistic responses if we discover a greater purpose to our troubles. Why is my work worth doing? Who will be helped if I respond well? Am I contributing to some greater good?

Of course, the work truly does have to contribute to something meaningful. People don't step forward in order to support greed or egotists or to benefit faceless entities such as shareholders. We need to know that our work contributes to helping other human beings. My favorite example of this desire to contribute was expressed in the mission statement created by employees at a facility that manufactured dog food. They expressed how their work was serving a greater good when they wrote, "Pets contribute to human health."

Use Rituals and Symbols

As shrines appear on streets mourning the dead and other demonstrations of grief flare on TV screens throughout this sorrowing world, we are becoming aware of the deep human need for shared symbolic expression when we experience something tragic. And also the need for celebration when we've experienced something wonderful.

The use of ritual and symbols is common in all cultures, although they almost disappeared in the United States until our lives became so stressful and isolatory. Now we are rediscovering this basic human behavior. Because it is so basic to humans, symbols and rituals appear spontaneously, even in organizations. No one department has to create them (a scary thought), but the organization *does* need to notice them when they appear, and to honor them by offering support and resources.

Pay Attention to Individuals

There is no substitute for direct, personal contact with employees. Even though managers are more stressed and have less time, it is crucial to pick up the phone and connect with those you want to retain. Personal conversations with key people, with experienced workers, with innovators, with those just joining the organization, with younger workers new to the workforce—all of these and more need to know that their leader is thinking about them. When people feel cared for, their stress is reduced and they contribute more to the organization. One of the key findings in the field of knowledge management is that people share their knowledge *only* when they feel cared for and when they care for the organization. It is not new technology that makes for knowledge exchanges but the quality of human relationships.

The Difficulty of Investing in Relationships

None of these suggested behaviors is new organizational advice. Most of us have had enough experience in organizations to know the importance of relationships. So why, as the storm clouds thicken, are we not investing in creating healthy, trusting relationships? One answer is that many organizations, as a matter of policy, deliberately distance themselves from their employees. They hold a dangerous assumption, which is that organizational flexibility is achieved by being able to let go of employees when times get hard. The ability to remain efficient is found primarily in the organization's ability to downsize staff. If you need to downsize, so the assumption goes, you don't want to know your employees or get personally involved with them.

What is most dangerous about this belief is that it is partly true. Organizations *do* need to be able to shrink and grow as times demand. But it is possible to achieve this workforce flexibility without sacrificing loyal, dedicated, and smart workers. Years ago, Harley-Davidson had to let go nearly 40 percent of its workforce. This was a wrenching but crucial decision for the survival of the company. However, the company took the time and paid attention to those individuals who were leaving and those who were staying. Every employee had a personal conversation with the CEO and received complete information about the company's circumstances. People understood why they were being let go, appreciated the personal conversation, and expressed their love and support for the company going forward. Over the years, many of those employees stayed in contact and were rehired as Harley prospered.

One Prediction about the Future

There is only one prediction about the future that I feel confident to make. During this period of random and unpredictable change, any organization that distances itself from its employees and refuses to cultivate meaningful relationships with them is destined to fail. Those organizations who will succeed are those that evoke our greatest human capacities—our need to be in good relationships, and our desire to contribute to something beyond ourselves. These qualities cannot be evoked through procedures and policies. They only are available in organizations where people feel trusted and welcome, and where people know that their work matters. The evidence is all around us, and here's one powerful story.

On September 11, the Federal Aviation Authority (FAA) cleared the skies of nearly 4,500 planes carrying 350,000 passengers in just a few hours. (Seventy-five percent of them landed within the first hour, more than one landing per second.) It was an unprecedented feat for the agency, one that had not been simulated since the end of the Cold War. And it was the first day on the job for the FAA official who gave the order to clear the skies. Controllers had to land these planes, while also staying vigilant for signs that any other planes had been hijacked. They succeeded through intense cooperation, absolute focus and dedication, and because they made decisions locally, including some that were outside policies. In the months following, officials started to try to capture this astonishing feat in new procedures, but then they scrapped the idea. One FAA official said, "A lot of things were done intuitively, things that you can't write down in a textbook or you can't train somebody to do." What is the FAA's policy and plan for preparing for another crisis of unknown dimensions? It will rely on the judgment, intuition, and commitment of its controllers and managers.

Leadership in Turbulent Times Is Spiritual

As our world grows more chaotic and unpredictable, leaders are asked questions for which their professional training did not prepare them.

> *How do I plan when I don't know what will happen next?*
> *How do I maintain my values when worldly temptations abound?*
> *Do I have a purpose to my life?*
> *Where can I find meaning in my life?*
> *Where can I find the courage and faith to stay the course?*

Humans have sought answers to these questions for as long as we've been around. It is a fundamental human characteristic to look at the circumstances of one's life and ask, "Why?" No matter how poor or desperate we are, we always need to assign a reason to *why* things are as they are. Every culture has its rituals and spiritual practices to answer this fundamental quest.

As our age has become more chaotic and complex, we've turned for answers to the contemporary god worshipped by Western culture, science. We've asked science to explain how to deal with chaos, catastrophes, and life's unpredictability. We want science to teach us how to prevent the sudden events that suddenly destroy lives and futures. We want science not just to explain chaos but to give us tools for controlling it. We want science to stop us from aging and dying and to get us out of all life's challenges.

But of course, this god of science can only fail us. Chaos can't be controlled; the unpredictable can't be predicted. Instead, we are being called to encounter life as it is: uncontrollable, unpredictable, messy, surprising, erratic. One of my own spiritual teachers commented, "The reason we don't like life is that it behaves like life."

I know that leaders today are faced with enormous challenges, most of them not of their own doing. As times grow more chaotic, as people question the meaning (and meaninglessness) of this life, people are clamoring for their leaders to save and rescue them. Historically, people often given away their freedom and allow dictatorship when confronted with uncertainty. People press their leaders to do anything to end the uncertainty, to make things better, to create stability. Even leaders who would never want to become dictators, those devoted to servant leadership, walk into this trap. They want to help, so they exert more control over the disorder. They try to create safety, to insulate people from the realities of change. They try to give answers to dilemmas that have no answers. No leader can achieve this, and it drains energy out of those who try.

Leadership through command and control is doomed to fail. No one can create sufficient stability and equilibrium for people to feel secure and safe. Instead, as leaders we must help people move into a relationship with uncertainty and chaos. Spiritual teachers have been doing this for millennia. Therefore, I believe that the times have led leaders to a spiritual threshold. We must enter the domain of spiritual traditions if we are to succeed as good leaders in these difficult times.

Why Leadership Is Spiritual Work

I believe that several principles describe the essential work for leaders in this era. I label this as "spiritual" work because each principle has been the focus of spiritual inquiry for centuries; these perspectives are found in nearly all spiritual traditions. It is in these traditions that we can find our answers.

Life Is Uncertain

How can we understand that change is just the way it is? In Buddhist thought, the source of true happiness comes from understanding this fact. Instead of holding on to any one thing or form, we expect that it will change. Good things, bad things—they come and go in this ever-changing world we live in. With this perspective it's easier to move on rather than cling desperately to old practices. But generally, we cling to what feels familiar until it no longer works for us. As a leader, it doesn't help to get angry when people cling to old ways. It's much more helpful to encourage people to reflect on their personal life experiences, to notice that they've changed many times in their life. People do know how to change. They also may notice that, at those times when they've let go and surrendered to uncertainty, they haven't died.

Life never stops teaching us about change. As leaders, hopefully we can be patient guides and coaches so that people discover their own experience with life's true nature.

Life Is Cyclical

Poet David Whyte has noted, "If you think life is always improving, you're going to miss half of it." Life is cyclical—we pass through different moods; we live through seasons; we have times of rich harvests and times of bleak winter. Life uses cycles to create newness. We move from the old to the new only if we let go.

Instead of fleeing from the fearful place of chaos or trying to rescue people from it, leaders can help people stay with the chaos, help them walk through it together, and look for the new insights and capacities that always emerge.

In Christian traditions, times of chaos have been called "dark nights of the soul." In our present culture, we call these "clinical depressions." I prefer the spiritual framing. In the dark night, we feel devoid of meaning, totally alone, abandoned by God. (Christian mystics believe that God consciously gives us these dark nights.) These dark times are the conditions for rebirth, for a new and stronger self to emerge. You probably have walked through many dark nights, and I encourage you to think how you changed, what new capacities you possessed when you emerged back into the light.

Meaning Is What Motivates People

Nothing motivates us humans more than meaning. I've seen many disillusioned and depressed staff groups develop high levels of energy and insight when they were asked to think about the meaning of their work. Consultant Kathy Dannemiller always asked groups to think about how the world would change because of the work they were doing. In such brutal times as these, when good work gets destroyed by events and decisions far beyond our influence, when we're so overwhelmed with tasks that we have no time to reflect, it is very important that the leader create time for people to remember *why* they're doing this work. What were we hoping to accomplish when we started this? Who are we serving by doing this work?

I have always been astonished by the deep meaning people ascribe to their work. Most people want their work to serve a greater good, to help other people. It doesn't matter what the work is; we'd rather be doing it in service to other people. In certain professions, such as health care, education, and non-profits, or whenever we feel "called" to our work, it is easier to remember the meaning of it. But we seldom have time to pause for a moment and remember the initial idealism and desire to serve that led us into our profession. However, our energy and rededication are only found there, in our ideals.

Service Brings Us Joy

Over the years, I've interviewed people who participated in disaster relief. I've always been astonished to notice that no matter how tragic and terrible the disaster, they always spoke of that experience with joy. They've led me to realize that there is nothing equal to helping other people. In service, we discover profound happiness. We all witnessed this in the days after September 11. As one survivor stated: "We didn't save ourselves. We tried to save each other."

The joy and meaning of service is found in every spiritual tradition. It has been expressed very simply in an ancient Buddhist teaching. "All happiness in the world comes from serving others; all sorrow in the world comes from acting selfishly."

Courage Comes from Our Hearts

Where do we find the courage to be leaders today? The etymology of the word *courage* gives the answer. *Courage* comes from the old French word for heart, *coeur*. When we are deeply affected, when our hearts respond to an issue or person, courage pours out from our open hearts. Please note that *courage* does not come from the root word for *analysis* or for *strategic planning*. We have to be engaged at the heart level in order to be courageous champions. As much as we may fear emotions at work, leaders need to be willing to let their hearts open and to tell stories that open other people's hearts.

We Are Interconnected with All Life

Every spiritual tradition speaks about oneness. So does new science. As leaders, we act on this truth when we're willing to notice how a decision might affect others, when we try and think systemically, when we're willing to look down the road and notice how, at this moment, we might be affecting future generations. Any act that takes us past the immediate moment, and past our self-protective ways, acknowledges that there's more to life than just us.

I learned a wonderfully simple way to think about our actions from a woman minister. She told how any time she makes a decision, she asks herself, "Is this decision going to bring people together? Will it weave a stronger web? Or will it create further disintegration and separation?" I like to ask another question as well: "In what I am about to do, am I turning toward others or turning away? Am I moving closer, or am I retreating from them?"

We Can Rely on Human Goodness

This is the first value of The Berkana Institute, the leadership foundation I cofounded in 1992. As Berkana does its work in the world, we rely on the great generosity and caring of humans. We know that there's more than enough human badness in the world, but the prevalence of badness only pushes us to rely even more on human goodness.

In your own leadership, what qualities of people do you rely on? I believe in these dark times that we can rely only on the hope, resiliency, and love that is found in the human spirit. Many people through history have suffered terribly, and many continue to suffer right now. Those we remember and admire— Helen Keller, Nelson Mandela, Ann Frank, war veterans, Holocaust survivors, genocide victims, cancer survivors—demonstrate what is best about us. We love to hear their stories because they illuminate what is good about being human. Vaclev Havel, the president of the Czech Republic, says that hope is not a result of the condition of our lives. It is fundamental to being human. (The state motto of South Carolina is similar: "If I breathe, I hope.")

We Need Peace of Mind

All spiritual traditions teach us ways to find peace of mind and acceptance. In the research on mind–body health, cultivating peace is a prerequisite for health. And who do we like to be around? Do we seek out angry or peaceful people? Do we find relief in noise or in quiet? As leaders, we need to find ways to help people work from a place of inner peace, even in the midst of turmoil. Frantic activity and fear only take us deeper into chaos. I've observed the power of starting a meeting with two minutes of silent contemplation. Or, when the meeting gets heated, of asking people to stop talking and just be silent for a minute. It's amazing how differently people come back into the fray if we've had those moments to pause.

Few of us want to work as frantically as we do; most of us hate meetings where tempers boil over. Brief moments of quiet can work wonders—silence is truly the pause that refreshes. Educator Parker Palmer tells of his initial discomfort at working in a Quaker organization, where they observed five minutes of contemplative silence before the start of every meeting. At one meeting, when there was a particularly contentious issue on the agenda, he was relieved to hear the leader announce that because of this serious issue, today they would not spend the first five minutes in silence. But then, to his dismay, he heard her announce, "Instead, we'll be silent for twenty minutes."

Attending to Your Personal Spiritual Health

I'd like to offer a few simple practices that I have found to be essential to maintain a sense of focus and peace as a leader.

Start the Day Off Peacefully

I've raised a large family, so I laugh as I state this. But I've learned that I can't expect to find peace at work. However peaceful I am as I leave my home, that's probably my peak peaceful experience of the day. So I have a strong motivation to find peace before I begin work. There are many ways to cultivate peace at the start of your day. You can drive to work in silence or listen to a particularly soothing piece of music. You can reflect on a spiritual phrase or parable. You can take a few minutes to just sit, either meditating or focusing on a lovely object. You can look for something beautiful outside your window. As your day grows crazier, it helps to know what peace feels like. Sometimes you can even recall that feeling in the midst of very great turmoil.

Learn to Be Mindful

Anytime you can keep yourself from instantly reacting, anytime you can pause for just a second, you are practicing mindfulness. Instead of letting your reactions and thoughts lead you, you step back and realize you can choose your reaction. Instead of being angry, you hesitate for a moment and realize you have other responses available. Instead of saying something hurtful, you pause and give yourself more options.

Slow Things Down

If you can't slow down a group or meeting, you can at least slow down yourself. I've learned to notice how I'm sitting. If I find myself leaning forward, moving aggressively into the discussion or argument, I force myself to sit back in the chair, even for just a moment. If I find my temper rising, I slow down and take just one deep breath. These are small things, but they yield big results.

Create Personal Measures

We all would prefer to be better people. We don't like to be angry or fearful or to be creating more problems for other people. But how can we know that we're succeeding in becoming people we respect? What are our personal measures? Some people create a measure such as telling fewer lies, or speaking the truth to people more often. Some notice when they are more patient or angry less often. I also use the question of "Am I turning toward or away?" as a personal measure of good behavior.

Expect Surprise

We're old enough now to know that life will keep interrupting our plans and surprising us at every turn of the way. It helps to notice this wisdom that we've been forced to acquire. Surprise is less traumatic once we accept it as a fact of life.

Practice Gratefulness

Most of us have been taught this, but how often do you take time, daily, to count your blessings? The wonder of this process is that as we take this daily inventory, we grow in gratefulness. We start to notice more and more—

people who helped us, grace that appeared, little miracles that saved us from danger. The daily practice of gratefulness truly changes us in wonderful ways. When you develop the practice of expressing your gratefulness to colleagues, your relationships improve dramatically.

I believe that, because you are human, you've already experienced the powers, fears, and joys that I've described. It is more important to access your own wisdom than to seek advice from anyone else. Life is a consistent teacher. It always teaches the same lessons. Change is just the way it is. Peace is not dependent on circumstances. We are motivated by meaning. We want to express our love through service. And when we believe that, as leaders, we are playing our part in something more purposeful than our small egos can ever explain, we become leaders who are peaceful, courageous, and wise.

The True Professional

The true professional is a person whose action points beyond
his or herself to that underlying reality,
that hidden wholeness, on which we all can rely.

Illusion

Too much of our action is really reaction. Such doing does not flow from
free and independent hearts
but depends on external provocation.

Such doing does not flow
it depends on external provocation.

It does not come from our sense of
who we are and what we want to do, but from

our anxious reading of how others define us
        our anxious reading of how others define us
                our anxious reading of how others define us

and of what the world demands.

        When we react in this way we do not act humanly.

The true professional is one
who does not obscure grace
with illusions of technical prowess,
the true professional is one
who strips away all illusions to reveal

a reliable truth
a reliable truth in which
the human heart can rest.

Can rest.

Unveil the illusions
unveil the illusions that
    masquerade
the illusions that masquerade
as reality and reveal
    the reality
    behind the masks.

    Catch the magician
deceiving us
    get a glimpse
        a glimpse of the
truth behind the trick.

    A glimpse.

Contemplation happens anytime we get a glimpse of the truth.

Action

Action, like a sacrament,
is the visible form of an invisible spirit
an outward manifestation of
an inward power.

> An expressive act is not to achieve a goal outside myself
> but to express a conviction
> a leading, a truth that is within me.

An expressive act is one taken
because if I did not
if I did not
if I did not take it
I would be denying
my own insight, gift, nature.

Action, like a sacrament, is the visible form of an invisible spirit
an outward manifestation of
an inward power. But as we act,
we not only express what is in us
and help give shape to the world.

We also receive what is outside us
and we reshape
> our inner selves.

When we act, the world acts back.

The world acts back
and we and the world,
we and the world are

co-created.

Right action is a process of birthing that cannot be forced
but only followed.

Surrender

When God's love for the world pierces our armor of fear
it is an awesome experience of calling and accountability.
When God's love pierces our armor of fear
it is awesome
it is awesome to be pierced by God
to be called to accountability
to be called by God's love
for the world.

The true professional is one
who does not obscure grace
with illusions of technical prowess,
the true professional is one
who strips away all illusions to reveal

a reliable truth in which
the human heart can rest.

Reveal a reliable truth.

Let our human hearts rest.

Note: This is a "found poem"—all phrases are taken from (i.e., found) in Parker Palmer's book *The Active Life*. I wrote this in tribute to Parker Palmer for the profound influence he's had on my work.

Obstacles
Where the Road Gets Hard

The Real Work of Knowledge Management
The Uses and Abuses of Measurement
Name, Connect, Nourish, Illuminate
Transforming Aggression into Creativity
Seven Hundred Years to Go

Each of these essays deals with some of the major and recurring obstacles that prevent us from putting a new worldview into action. Some of these essays were written in the 1990s, but our struggles to get over these hurdles have only intensified as we continue to apply the wrong paradigm. Living systems provides key insights and processes that dissolve many of these difficulties. The last essay on "Transforming Aggression" draws not from new science but from ancient wisdom. It is an adaptation of a process taught for eons in Tibetan Buddhism.

After so many years of defending ourselves against life and searching for better controls, we sit exhausted in the unyielding structures of organization we've created, wondering what happened. What happened to effectiveness, to creativity, to meaning? What happened to us? Trying to get these structures to change becomes the challenge of our lives. We draw their futures and design them into clearly better forms. We push them, we prod them. We try fear, we try enticement. We collect tools, we study techniques. We use everything we know and end up nowhere. What happened?

—Margaret Wheatley and Myron Kellner-Rogers,
A Simpler Way

The Real Work of
Knowledge Management

We really do live in the Information Age, a revolutionary era when the availability of information is changing everything. Nothing is the same since the world was networked together and information became instantly accessible. Information has destroyed boundaries, borders, boxes, distance, values, roles, and rules. The availability of information has dissolved the walls of repressive governments, dishonest executives, and it has the potential to create the greatest mass empowerment of all time.

Because of access to information, we are in new relationships with everyone: with medical doctors (we go to the Web and learn more than they do,) with car salesmen (we know the real sticker price,) and with leaders of all kinds (we know when they walk their talk). The World Wide Web has created a world that is transparent, volatile, sensitive to the least disturbance, and choked with rumors, misinformation, truths, and passions.

This webbed world has changed the way we work and live. The notion of 24/7/365 is one consequence of instant access and the dissolution of boundaries. We no longer have clear lines between work and private life—if the cell phone is on and there's an Internet connection available, bosses and colleagues expect us to be available. Increasingly, it's impossible to "turn off," to find time to think, to take time to develop relationships, to even ask colleagues how they're doing.

Information has changed capitalism and the fundamental character of corporate life. Corporations now play in the global casino—focused on numbers moment to moment, suffering instant losses or gains in trading, merging to look powerful, downsizing to look lean, bluffing and spin doctoring to stay in the game. In this casino environment, long-term has disappeared, thinking for the future is impossible, and developing an organization that will still be around in twenty years can seem like a sentimental and wasteful activity.

These are only a few of the profound changes created by the Information Age. A September 2000 study by a futures group from the U.S. military summed it up this way: "The accelerated pace and grand breadth of information exchange is *arguably beyond comprehension and certainly out of control*. With so much information to choose from, each day it becomes harder to determine what is real, right, and relevant to peoples' lives" (ASAF Institute, 2000).

Knowledge Management Is a Survival Skill

In this time of profound chaos and newness, we still have to do our work. But what is our work? For those in human resources information management, there is relentless pressure to find ways for technology and people to support organizations through this tumultuous time. Organizations need to be incredibly smart, fast, agile, responsive. They need to respond and make smart decisions at ever-increasing speed, even as the unintended consequences of speedy decisions flare up in a nanosecond and keep leaders focused only on firefighting. The old days of "continuous improvement" seem as leisurely as a picnic from the past. In this chaotic and complex twenty-first century, the pace of evolution has entered warp speed, and those who can't learn, adapt, and change moment to moment simply won't survive.

Many of these organizational needs are bundled together today under the banner of *knowledge management*. The organization that knows how to convert information into knowledge, that knows what it knows, that can act with greater intelligence and discernment—these are the organizations that will make it into the future. We all know that our organizations need to be smarter. Knowledge management (KM) therefore should be something eagerly accepted by leaders; it should be an incredibly easy sell. Yet KM appears at a time when all organizations are battered and bruised by so much change, entering the Information Age after decades of fads, and by investments in too many organizational change efforts that failed to deliver what was promised. These experiences have exhausted us all, made many cynical, and left others of us worried that we'll never learn how to create organizations that can thrive in this century.

Unlike past organizational change efforts, knowledge management is truly a survival issue. Done right, it can give us what we so desperately need—organizations that act with intelligence. Done wrong, we will, like lemmings, keep rushing into the future without using our intelligence to develop longer-term individual and organizational capacity. To continue blindly down our current path, where speed and profits are the primary values, where there is no time to think or relate, is suicidal.

Beliefs That Prevent Knowledge Management

How can we ensure that KM doesn't fail or get swept aside as just the most recent fad? How can we treasure it for the life-saving process it truly could be? For knowledge management to succeed, we will need to lay aside these dangerously out-of-date beliefs:

— *Organizations are machines.* This belief becomes visible every time we create separate parts—tasks, roles, functions—and engineer (and reengineer) them to achieve predetermined performance levels. It is the manager's role to manage the parts to achieve those outcomes. Strangely, we also act as though people are machines. We attempt to "reprogram" people with new training and technology, hoping that, like good robots, they will go off and do exactly what they're told. When people resist being treated as dumb machines, we criticize them as "resistant to change."

— *Only material things are real.* A great deal of our efforts focus on trying to make invisible "things" (such as knowledge, commitment, trust, relationships) assume material form. We believe we have accomplished this when we assign numbers to them. This belief combines with the next one:

— *Only numbers are real.* This belief is ancient, dating back to the sixth century B.C.E. Once we assign a number to something (a grade in school; a performance measure; a statistic), we relax and feel we have adequately described what's going on. These two beliefs reinforce that . . .

— *You can only manage what you can measure.* We use numbers to manage everything: ROI; P/E ratios; inventory returns; employee morale; staff turnover. If we can't assign a number to it, we don't pay it any attention. To keep track of increasingly complex measurements, we turn to our favorite new deity, which is the belief that . . .

— *Technology is always the best solution.* We have increasing numbers of problems, which we try to solve using technology. But this reliance on technology actually only increases our problems. We don't notice that the numeric information we enter in a computer cannot possibly describe the complexity of the experience or person we are trying to manage. By choosing computers (and numbers) as our primary management tool, we set ourselves up for guaranteed and repeated failures.

All of these beliefs show up strongly in knowledge management. We're trying to manage something—knowledge—that is inherently invisible, incapable of being quantified, and born in relationships, not statistics. And we are relying on technology to solve our problems with KM—we focus on constructing the right database, its storage and retrieval system, and assume we have KM solved.

The Japanese approach KM differently than we do in the West. The difference in approach exposes these Western beliefs with great clarity. In the West, we have focused on explicit knowledge—knowledge one can see and document—instead of dealing with the much more important but intangible realm of "tacit" knowledge, knowledge that is very present, but only observable in the doing, not as a number. American and European efforts have been focused on developing measures for and assigning values to knowledge. Once we had the numbers, we assumed we could manage it, even though more and more people now acknowledge that "knowledge management" is an oxymoron.

Current approaches to KM in the West demonstrate that we believe that knowledge is a thing, a material substance that can be produced, measured, catalogued, warehoused, traded, and shipped. The language of KM is littered with this "thing" thinking. We want to "capture" knowledge, to inventory it, to push it into or pull it out from people. One British expert on KM, David Skyrme (www.skyrme.com), reports that in both Britain and the United States, a common image of KM is of "decanting the human capital into the structural capital of an organization." I don't know how this imagery affects you, but I personally don't want to have my head opened, my cork popped, my entire body tilted sideways so that what I know pours out of me into an organizational vat. This prospect is not what motivates me to notice what I know or to share it.

These language choices have serious implications. They reveal that we think knowledge is an entity, something that exists independent of person or context, capable of being moved about and manipulated for organizational advantage. We need to abandon this language and, more important, the beliefs that engender it. We need to look at knowledge—its creation, transfer, its very nature—with new eyes. As we rethink what we know about knowledge and how we handle the challenges of knowledge in organizations, our most important work is to pay serious attention to what we always want to ignore: *the human dimension.*

Think, for a moment, about what you know about knowledge, not from a theoretical or organizational perspective but from your own experience. In myself, I notice that knowledge is something I create because I am *in relationship—*

relating to another person, an event, or an idea. Something pulls me outside myself and forces me to react. As I figure out what's going on or what something means, I develop interpretations that make sense to me. Knowledge is something I create inside myself through my engagement with the world. Knowledge never exists independently of this process of my being in relationship with an event, an idea, or another person. This process is true for all of us. Knowledge is created in relationship, inside thinking, reflecting human beings.

From biology, it is evident that we are not the only life form that engages in knowledge creation. Everything alive learns and creates knowledge for its survival. All living beings pay exquisite attention to what's going on in their environment, with their neighbors, offspring, predators, and even the weather. They notice something and then decide whether they need to adapt and change. Living beings never engage in this process of noticing-reacting-changing because some boss tells them to do it. Every form of life is free to decide what to pay attention to and how to respond. Individuals decide how they will respond to their neighbors and to current conditions, and then they live or die as a result of their decisions.

This same autonomy describes us humans, but we tend to find it problematic if we're the boss. We give staff detailed directions and policies on how to do something, and then they, like all life, use their autonomy to change it in some way. They fine-tune it; they adapt it to their unique context; they add their own improvements to how the task gets done. If we're the one in charge, however, we don't see this behavior as creativity. We label it as resistance or disobedience. But what we are seeing is *new knowledge*. People have looked at the directive, figured out what would work better in the present context, and created a new way of doing it, one that, in most cases, stands more chance of success.

I experienced this knowledge creation process months ago as I sat on an air-port commuter bus and listened to the driver train a newly hired employee. For thirty minutes I eavesdropped as she energetically revealed the secrets and efficiencies she had discovered for how to get to the airport in spite of severe traffic or bad weather. She wasn't describing company policy. She was giving a nonstop, virtuoso performance of what she had invented and changed in order to get her customers to their destination. I'm sure her supervisor had no idea of any of this new knowledge she'd been creating on each bus ride.

But this bus driver is typical. People develop better ways of doing their work all the time and also like to brag about it. In survey after survey, workers report that most of what they learn about their job, they learn from informal conversations. They also report that they *frequently* have ideas for improving work but don't tell their bosses because they don't believe their bosses care.

Some Principles That Facilitate Knowledge Management

Knowledge creation is natural to life, and wanting to share what we know is humanly satisfying. So what's the problem? In organizations, what sends these behaviors underground? Why do workers go dumb? Why do we fail to manage knowledge? Here are a few principles that I believe lead to answers to these questions.

Knowledge Is Created by Human Beings

If we want to succeed with KM, then we must stop thinking of people as machines. Instead, we must attend to human needs and dynamics. Perhaps if we renamed it "human knowledge," we would remind ourselves of what it is and where it comes from. We would refocus our attention on the organiza-tional conditions that support people, that foster relationships, that give people time to think and reflect. We would stop fussing with the hardware; we would cease trying to find more efficient means to "decant" us. We would notice that when we speak of such things as "assets" or "intellectual capital" that it is not knowledge that is the asset or capital. People are.

It Is Natural for People to Create and Share Knowledge

We have forgotten many important truths about human motivation. Study after study confirms that people are motivated by work that provides growth, recognition, meaning, and good relationships. We want our lives to mean something; we want to contribute to others; we want to learn; we want to be together. And we need to be involved in decisions that affect us. If we believed these studies and created organizations that embodied them, then work would be far more productive and enjoyable. We would discover that people can be filled with positive energy. Organizations would be overwhelmed by new knowledge, innovative solutions, and great teamwork. It is essential that we begin to realize that human nature is the blessing, not the problem. As a species, we are actually very good to work with.

Everybody Is a Knowledge Worker

This statement was an operating principle of one of my clients. If everybody is assumed to be creating knowledge, then the organization takes responsibility for supporting all its workers, not just a special few. It makes certain that everyone has easy access to anyone, anywhere in the organization, because you never know who has already invented the solution you need. The Japanese learned this and demonstrated it in their approach to KM. I learned it on that bus ride.

People Choose to Share Their Knowledge

This is an extremely important statement, and the important word is *choose*. Most KM programs get stuck because individuals will not share their knowledge. But it's important to remember that people are making a choice not to share what they know. They *willingly share* if they feel committed to the organi-

zation, believe their leaders are worth supporting, feel encouraged to participate and learn, and value their colleagues. Knowledge sharing is going on all the
time in most organizations. Every organization is filled with self-organized communities of practice, relationships that people spontaneously create among colleagues to help them work more effectively or to help them survive the current
turbulence. These communities of practice are evidence of people's willingness
to learn and to share what they know. But the organization must provide the
right conditions to support people's willingness. Some of these necessary, non-
negotiable conditions are:

— people must understand and value the objective or strategy,
— people must understand how their work adds value to the common objective,
— people must feel respected and trusted,
— people must know and care about their colleagues, and
— people must value and trust their leaders.

If we contrast this list to the current reality in most organizations, it becomes
obvious how much work is needed to create the conditions for effective KM.
This is a proven list, with more than enough case studies and research to vali-
date it. If we don't vigorously undertake creating these conditions as the real
work of KM, then we might as well stop wasting everyone's time and money
and just abandon KM right now.

Knowledge Management Is Not about Technology
This would seem obvious from the preceding statements, but it feels important
to stress because we modern managers are dazzled by technical solutions. If
people aren't communicating, we just create another Web site or online conference; if we want to harvest what people know, we just create an inventoried
database; if we're geographically dispersed, we just put video cams on people's
desks. But these technical solutions don't solve a thing if other aspects of the
culture—the human dimension—are ignored.

A few years ago, British Petroleum successfully used desktop video cams to facilitate knowledge sharing among it offshore oil drilling rigs. But this wasn't *all* it did. It also worked simultaneously to create a culture that recognized individual contribution and moved aggressively to create a new vision that employees could rally behind (BP became "Beyond Petroleum").

Many organizations have learned from experience that if they want productive teams, they must bring people together in the same space several times a year. They're learning that in the absence of face-to-face meetings, people have a hard time sharing knowledge. It's important to remember that technology does not connect us. Our *relationships* connect us, and once we know the person or team, then we use the technology to stay connected. We share knowledge because we are in relationship, not because we have broader bandwidth available.

Knowledge Is Born in Chaotic Processes That Take Time
The irony of this principle is that it demands two things we don't have: a tolerance for messy, nonlinear processes, and time. But creativity is only available when we become confused and overwhelmed, when we get so frustrated that we admit we don't know. And then, miraculously, a perfect insight appears, suddenly. This is how great scientists achieve breakthrough discoveries, how teams and individuals discover transforming solutions. Great insights never appear at the end of a series of incremental steps. Nor can they be commanded to appear on schedule, no matter how desperately we need them. They present themselves only after a lot of work that culminates in so much frustration that we surrender. Only then are we humble enough and tired enough to open ourselves to entirely new solutions. They leap into view suddenly (the "aha" experience), always born in messy processes that take time.

Self-awareness and reflection are increasingly listed as critical leadership skills. Some companies created architectural spaces to encourage informal conversations, mental spaces to encourage reflection, and learning spaces to encourage journal writing and other reflective thought processes. These innovations, however, run contrary to the prevailing tendencies for instant answers and breathless decision making. Too many of these sensible innovations fail because warp speed asserts its demands. People simply don't have time to use their journals or to sit in conversation-friendly spaces.

We have to face the difficult fact that until we claim time for reflection, until we make space for thinking, we won't be able to generate knowledge, or to know what knowledge we already possess. We can't argue with the clear demands of knowledge creation—it requires time to develop. It matures inside human relationships.

Although we live in a world completely revolutionized by information, it is important to remember that it is *knowledge* we are seeking, not information. Unlike information, knowledge involves us and our deeper motivations and dynamics as human beings. We interact with something or someone in our environment and then use who we are—our history, our identity, our values, habits, beliefs—to decide what the information means. In this way, through our construction, information becomes knowledge. Knowledge is always a reflection of who we are, in all our uniqueness. It is impossible to disassociate *who* is creating the knowledge from the knowledge itself.

It would be good to remember this as we proceed with knowledge management. We can put down the decanting tools, we can stop focusing all our energy on database designs, and we can get on with the real work. We must recognize that knowledge is everywhere in the organization, but we won't have access to it until, and only when, we create work that is meaningful, leaders that are trustworthy, and organizations that foster everyone's contribution and support by giving staff time to think and reflect together.

This is the real work of knowledge management. It requires clarity and courage—and in stepping into it, we will be contributing to the creation of a far more intelligent and hopeful future than the one presently looming on the horizon.

The Uses and Abuses of Measurement

with **Myron Rogers**

In the West, we live in a culture that is crazy about numbers. Starting in the sixth century B.C.E., numbers became the means we used to see reality. But over time, numbers became the only reality. Today, we make something real by assigning a number to it. Once it's a number, it's ours to manage and control. The poet W. H. Auden years ago wrote about this Western obsession: "And still they come, new from those nations to which the study of that which can be weighed and measured is a consuming love."

The search for measures has taken over the world as the primary means to control systems and people. We depend on numbers to know how we're doing for virtually everything. We ascertain our health with numbers. How many calories or carbs should I eat? What's my cholesterol reading? We assess people with numbers. What's your IQ? Your EQ? Your GPA? And of course we judge organizational viability with numbers. We manage organizations by metrics to the extent that one executive, when trying to understand a company he had just bought, asked only to see "the pile of metrics you use to run this place."

Numbers are the "hard stuff," the real world of management—graphs, charts, indices, ratios. Everyone knows that "you can only manage what you can measure." The work of modern managers is to interpret and manipulate these numerical views of reality. Many good managers have been compelled to become earnest students of measurement. But are measures and numbers the right pursuit? Do these measures make for enduring organizations? And what effects has this measurement mania created?

Instead of assuming that numbers are the solution, consider this question: What are the problems in organizations for which we assume measures are the solution? Assumably, most managers want reliable, quality work. They want people to perform better. They want accountability, focus, teamwork, and quality.

If you agree that these are the general behaviors you're seeking, ask whether, in your experience, you've been able to find measures that *sustain* these important behaviors over time. If you haven't found useful measures yet, are you or your organization still expecting to find them, rotating through different vendors to find the ultimate metric or instrument? Is measurement still believed to be the way to elicit quality performance?

The problem is that these behaviors are never produced by measurement. They are performance capabilities that emerge as people feel connected to their work and to each other. They are capacities that emerge as colleagues develop a shared sense of what they want to work on, and as they work in an environment where everyone feels welcome to contribute to that shared purpose.

Each of these qualities and behaviors—accountability, focus, teamwork, quality—is a choice that people make. Depending on how connected they feel to the organization or team, they choose to pay attention, to take responsibility, to innovate, to learn and share their learnings. People can't be punished or paid into these behaviors. Either they are contributed or withheld by individuals as *they choose* whether and how they will work with us. Every employee, in this sense, is a volunteer.

But to look at prevailing organizational practices, most managers consistently choose measurement as the route to these capacities. They agonize to find the right reward to tie to the right measure. How long have organizations searched for rewards that will result in better teamwork or more innovation? And haven't leaders noticed that if they find an effective external reward, it only works as an incentive in the short term, if at all? Ironically, the longer we try to cultivate these behaviors through measurement and reward, the more damage we do to the quality of our relationships, the more we trivialize the meaning of work, and the more disengaged people become.

Far too many organizations have lost the path to quality because they have burdened themselves with unending measures. Too many employees have become experts at playing "the numbers game" to satisfy bosses rather than becoming experts at their jobs. Pursuing measurement as the primary means of motivating people leads us dangerously far from the organizational qualities and behaviors that we require.

But measurement is critical. It can provide something that is essential to sustenance and growth: feedback. All life thrives on feedback and dies without it. We have to know what is going on around us, how our actions impact others, how the environment is changing, how we're changing. If we don't have access to this kind of information, we can't adapt or grow. Without feedback, we shrivel into routines and develop hard shells that keep newness out. We don't survive for long.

In any living system, feedback differs from measurement in several significant ways:

— *Feedback is self-generated*. An individual and a system notice whatever they determine is important for them. They ignore everything else.

— *Feedback depends on context*. The critical information is being generated right now. Failing to notice the "now," or staying stuck in past assumptions, is very dangerous.

— Feedback changes. What an individual or system chooses to notice will change depending on the past, the present, and the future. Looking for information only within rigid categories leads to blindness, which is very dangerous.

— New and surprising information can get in. The boundaries are permeable.

— Feedback is life sustaining. It provides essential information about how to maintain one's existence. It also indicates when adaptation and growth are necessary.

— Feedback develops fitness. Through the constant exchange of information, the individual and its environment coevolve toward mutual sustainability.

As we reflect on the capacities that feedback can provide, it seems we are seeking many similar attributes in our organizations. But we haven't replicated the same processes, and therefore we can't achieve the same outcomes. There are some critical distinctions between feedback and measurement, as evident in the following contrasts.

Some Important Distinctions

Feedback	Measurement
Context-dependent	*One size fits all.*
Self-determined. The system chooses what to notice.	*Imposed. Criteria are established externally.*
Information is accepted from anywhere	*Information is put in fixed categories*
The system creates own meaning.	*Meaning is predetermined.*
Newness, surprise are essential.	*Prediction, routine are valued.*
The focus is on adaptability and growth.	*The focus is on stability and control.*
Meaning evolves.	*Meaning remains static.*
The system coadapts with its environment.	*The system adapts to the measures.*

If we understand the critical role played by feedback in living systems and contemplate these distinctions, we could develop measurement processes that support the behaviors and capacities we require, that enhance the vitality and adaptability of the organization. To create measures that more closely resemble feedback, we suggest the following questions. These are useful design criteria for developing measures and measurement processes.

— *Who gets to create the measures?* Measures are meaningful and important only when generated by those doing the work. Any group can benefit from others' experience and from experts, but the final measures need to be their creation. People only support what they create, and those closest to the work know the most about what is significant to measure.

— *How will we measure our measures?* How can we keep measures useful and current? What will indicate that they are now obsolete? How will we keep abreast of changes in context that warrant new measures? Who will look for the unintended consequences that accompany any process and feed that information back to us?

— *Are we designing measures that are permeable rather than rigid?* Are they open enough? Do they invite in newness and surprise? Do they encourage people to look in new places or to see with new eyes?

— *Will these measures create information that increases our capacity to develop, to grow the purpose of this organization?* Will this particular information help individuals, teams, and the entire organization grow in the right direction? Will this information help us know whether we are achieving our stated purpose?

— *What measures will inform us about critical capacities—accountability, learning, teamwork, quality, and innovation?* How will we measure these essential behaviors without destroying them through the assessment process? What ways of measuring support the relationships that give rise to these important behaviors?

If these questions seem daunting, please be assured they are not difficult to implement. But they do require extraordinary levels of participation—defining and using measures becomes everyone's responsibility. In our consulting, we've known teams, manufacturing plants, and service organizations where everyone knew that measurement was critical to their success and went at the task of measuring with great enthusiasm and creativity. They were aggressive about seeking information from anywhere that might contribute to those purposes they had defined as most important to their organization, such things as safety, team-based organization, or social responsibility. Their process was creative, experimental, and the measures they developed were often nontraditional. People stretched and struggled to find ways to measure qualitative aspects of work. They developed unique and complex multivariate formulas that would work for a while and then would be replaced by new ones.

They understood that the right measurements gave them access to the information they needed to prosper and grow. But what was "right" kept changing. And in contrast to most organizations, measurement felt alive and vital in these work environments. It wasn't a constraint or deadening weight; rather, it helped people accomplish what they wanted to accomplish. It provided feedback, the information necessary for them to adapt and thrive.

Being in these workplaces, we also learned that measurement needs to serve the deepest purposes of work. It is only when we connect at the level of purpose that we willingly offer ourselves to the organization. When we have connected to the possibilities of what we might create together, then we want to gather information that will help us be better contributors.

But in too many organizations, just the reverse happens. The measures define what is meaningful rather than letting the greater meaning of the work define the measures. As the focus narrows, people disconnect from any larger purpose, and only do what is required of them. They become focused on meeting the petty requirements of measurement and, eventually, they die on the job. They end up playing a numbers game and lose motivation to do good work.

If we look closely at the experience of the past few years, it is clear that as a management culture, we have succeeded at developing finer and more sophisticated measures. But has this sophistication at managing by the numbers led to the levels of performance or commitment we've been seeking? And if we have achieved good results in these areas, was it because we discovered the right measures, or was something else going on in the life of the organization?

We would like to dethrone measurement from its godly position, to reveal the false god it has been. We want instead to offer measurement a new job—that of helpful *servant*. We want to use measurement to give us the kind and quality of feedback that supports and welcomes people to step forward with their desire to contribute, to learn, and to achieve. We want measurement to be used from a deeper place of understanding, the understanding that the real capacity of an organization arises when colleagues willingly struggle together in a common work that they find meaningful.

Name, Connect, Nourish, Illuminate: Supporting Pioneering Leaders

How would you describe these times? Is it a time of increasing economic and political instability, of growing divisiveness and fear, of failing systems and dying dreams? Is it a time of new possibilities, of great examples of hope, of positive human evolution, of transformation? Are we succeeding in solving major problems, or are we creating more? Is it any of these things? Is it all of these things?

It's important to think about how we answer these questions, because those answers affect our choice of actions. If we think that, generally, things are working, that at present we're going through a difficult but temporary downturn, then we don't question current systems or their operating assumptions. Instead, we work hard to revive and improve them. We support initiatives and programs focused on *process improvements*, developing present systems to work more effectively and more efficiently.

If we believe that the old system cannot be repaired, if we expect to see only more system failures, then the work is not to fix. Instead, support needs to be given to radically different processes and methods, new systems based on new assumptions. The work becomes not process improvement but process revolution.

What time is it?

TRAJECTORY OF THE HEALTH OF PRESENT SYSTEMS

PRESENT TIME

CAN THEY BE FIXED?

WILL THEY CONTINUE TO FAIL?

Where Have All the Leaders Gone?

There is a well-noted and alarming trend reported throughout the world—a desperate shortage of good leaders and talented professionals. These shortages appear at a time when the world is reeling from years of failed leadership. Leaders either have struggled valiantly with ineffective means, such as bureaucracy and command and control, or have held onto power through brutal and corrupt means.

This legacy of bad leadership continues today. In response to this era's increasing turbulence, too many leaders grasp desperately for power. Daily, we hear of corruption, extremes of abuse, and belligerent behaviors on the part of leaders.

Yet other leaders attempt to respond to the crises of these times with courage and vision. They want to resolve the most pressing problems of this time: health, human rights, poverty, hunger, illiteracy, environmental issues, democracy. But their well-intentioned efforts often are subverted by a lack of skillful means. Money for projects disappears because of inexperience and mismanagement. Change efforts fail because of poor implementation processes. In developing countries we say there's a leadership vacuum. In developed countries, we ask, "Where have all the leaders gone?"

So the need for new leadership is urgent. It is needed in communities everywhere. We need leaders who know how to nourish and rely on the innate creativity, freedom, generosity, and caring of people. We need leaders who are life affirming rather than life destroying. Unless we quickly figure out how to nurture and support this new leadership, we can't hope for peaceful change. We will, instead, be confronted by increasing anarchy and societal meltdowns.

Thus, new leadership becomes a central and pressing challenge of our time.

The Story of CIDA City Campus, South Africa

A few years ago, I met a remarkable South African leader, Taddy Blecher. Together with his colleagues and many professionals who volunteer their time, he has created the most amazing university in Johannesburg—CIDA City Campus. In existence for just a few years, CIDA already serves several thousand students from the poorest rural areas in South Africa. Each entering class, of about one thousand students, is chosen from several thousand applicants, and the selection is done by current students.

Taddy has an unshakable belief in the potential of people: "Everyone is a leader and needs to be cherished for that." At CIDA, thousands of young students are developing into new leaders for South Africa. Nothing about CIDA resembles traditional models of education. Instead, they rely on the deep communitarian values of Africa. One thousand students take the same class and the same exams at the same time. They live together in formerly high-class, now-abandoned hotels in downtown Johannesburg. They advise each other, look out for each other, go job hunting together, sing together, cook together. They live, work, and study as a community. In this community, no one struggles alone, and no one succeeds at the expense of another. CIDA students outperform traditional students academically and in the workplace, and they radiate belief in themselves and their potential to serve their nation.

They also know how to manifest their leadership with exponential power. When I visited CIDA, I met a group of thirty students who had been specially trained in AIDS awareness education and then gone back to their rural villages to teach their communities about HIV/AIDS. Each student had pledged to visit with one thousand people. They had just returned from this weekend effort and proudly announced that they had brought AIDS education to thirty thousand villagers in four days. Another group was about to be trained to educate local people in how to handle their money, credit, and banking.

The enthusiasm and joy that radiate at CIDA stand in stark contrast to other educational institutions. But rather than treat CIDA as an interesting exception to the norm, I want to illuminate it as representative of our future. The young leaders developing at CIDA demonstrate how much more powerful idealism can be when held in community, how serving others is a source of joy and energy, how together we might possibly change the world. No one at CIDA acts in isolation. Working together in supportive community, each develops their unique skills and capacity as a leader. And they sustain their enthusiasm for leadership at a time when the problems faced by their nation and the African continent are overwhelming and seemingly without solution.

The New Leaders Are Already Here

Not only at CIDA but everywhere, there are aspiring leaders who have a firm commitment to lead in new ways, to not repeat the mistakes and abuses of the past. They exist in all communities, clear in their resolve to lead differently. They often say that leadership has chosen them, that it is their *vocation* to lead at this time. But they are trying to forge new leadership while living in countries and communities characterized by either corrupt leaders or well-intentioned bureaucrats. From whom can they learn new ways? Who are their mentors? How can they quickly learn alternative modes of leadership? And if they've grown up under oppression and colonialism, told for centuries that they're worthless and powerless, how do they let go of that conditioning and truly empower themselves as leaders?

I strongly believe that the old leadership paradigm has failed us and that our current systems will continue to unravel. This has changed what I do and whom I choose to support. I no longer spend any time trying to fix or repair the old or to improve old leadership methods. I spend all of my time now sup- porting those giving birth to the new, those pioneering with new approaches to organizing and leading. In communities all over the world, many brave pioneers are experimenting with new approaches for resolving the most difficult societal problems. These new leaders have abandoned traditional practices of hierarchy, power, and bureaucracy. They believe in people's innate creativity and caring. They know that most people can be awakened to be active in determining what goes on in their communities and organizations. They practice consistent innovation and courage—wherever they see a problem, they also see possibility. They figure out how to respond. If one response doesn't work, they try another. They naturally think in terms of interconnectedness, following problems wherever they lead, addressing multiple causes rather than single symptoms. They think in terms of complex global systems yet also work locally.

The Challenges of Paradigm Pioneers

Pioneering leaders face very challenging conditions. They act in isolation, are often criticized, mocked, or ignored by the prevailing culture. They have no way of knowing that they are not along, that there are many pioneers struggling to discover new ways of leading. In the midst of such criticism and loneliness, it is a constant struggle to maintain focus and courage.

And, there are other serious challenges for these pioneers, those that happen when people are confronted with a new worldview.

— *New leaders must invent the future while dealing with the past.* In speaking with these new leaders, it is very clear that they refuse to carry the past into the future. They do not want to repeat the mistakes of the past having, in many cases, personally suffered from ineffective or brutal leadership. They want to work in new ways, but these new ways of organizing, the new processes for implementing change, have yet to be developed. So they do double duty. They must invent new processes and organizing forms, and simultaneously also solve the complex problems of this time.

— *It is difficult to break with tradition. It is not easy to invent the new.* It is difficult to break free of the training, history, and familiar practices of the prevailing culture. New leaders certainly know that bureaucracy doesn't work, that corruption destroys communities, that aid administered from the top down most often fails. They refuse to repeat these practices, but they, like all of us, have been raised in these traditional ways. Past habits of practice exert strong pressures. When crises mount and people feel fearful and overwhelmed, we default back to practices that are familiar, even if they are ineffective.

— *Supporters want them to look familiar.* Those with the means to support new leadership often complicate their pioneering work by insisting that they use familiar and traditional leadership processes. Those with resources often feel it's too risky to support experiments with new practices. It feels safer to ask for traditional strategic plans, business plans, measurements, and frequent reports, no matter what the context of the initiative. On the surface these seem to be important skill sets, but there is now substantial research demonstrating the failure of these methods to produce desired results in the most traditional organizations. Perhaps supporters are risk-averse; perhaps they are unaware that these methods don't work. Whatever the reason, sponsors insist that pioneering leaders conform to the past. Resources are not available unless new leaders can demonstrate competency in familiar leadership practices, even those that have consistently failed to achieve sustained change.

And when there is competition for scarce resources, it is easy for pioneers to lose their way. Against their best judgment of what works in their community, they agree to comply with procedures and practices they know can't succeed. Over time, they fail, not from lack of vision or willingness to experiment but because they have been held back from those experiments. We destroy these pioneers by insisting that they conform to the mistakes of the past.

– There is no room for failure. As pioneers, it is impossible to get it right the first time. No one has yet drawn the accurate maps—explorers learn as they go. Our present culture doesn't support this kind of experimentation. We want answers quickly; we ask people to demonstrate success early in their ventures. We evaluate them based on short-term measures. We seldom give adequate time for the explorations and failures that are part of mapping a new territory. Instead of offering additional resources to their explorations and experiments, we abandon them in favor of safer projects that employ familiar, flawed means.

Paradigm pioneers struggle in isolation to create
the new in the context of the old.

– We want them to fail. This is the greatest, unspoken challenge facing pioneering leaders. Society does not want them to succeed. If we acknowledge their success, it means we will have to change. We will have to abandon the comfort of our familiar beliefs and practices. Even as the old ways fail, we hold onto them more fiercely and apply them more zealously.

In his seminal work on paradigms, Thomas Kuhn described the behavior of scientists when confronted with evidence that pointed to a new worldview. When the new evidence clearly demonstrated the need for a change in paradigms, scientists were observed working hard to make the evidence conform to their old worldview. In defense of the old, they would discard or reinterpret the data. (This was always done unconsciously.) And in the most startling instances, they actually would be blind to the new information—even with the data in front of them, they literally could not see it. For them, the new did not exist.

When the paradigm is changing, it is common to experience each of these dynamics. How often do we see an innovative approach, and then characterize it as traditional? How often do we observe new leadership practices and deny their existence? How often do we treat their successes as anomalies or as exceptions to the norm? How difficult is it for us to acknowledge them for what they are, radical departures from tradition, the first trail markers of our way to the future?

Mohammed Junus, the founder of Grameen Bank in Bangladesh and pioneer of microlending to the poor, tells the story of trying to get support from traditional bankers for his first loans to poor people. Junus wanted to loan very small amounts of money (often not more than a few dollars) to give Bangla people the means to start their own businesses. Whatever evidence he presented, the bank's reply was always the same: "The poor are not credit-worthy." Frustrated, he then loaned his own money to the poor and was paid back on time. But the bank's response was the same. Even after several years of successful lending to the poor, Junus still encountered the same old belief: "The poor are not credit-worthy." He realized that no matter how much evidence he might accumulate to demonstrate the contrary, the banks would never see his evidence or change their beliefs. (Grameen has since loaned many millions to the poor and developed a model for microlending that is used worldwide.

Learning Occurs in Community

Because of the world's pressing leader shortage and these paradigm-shift dynamics, there is an urgent need to support, strengthen, and nurture pioneering new leaders. They are eager learners, willing to try new approaches, hungry for methods and ideas that will work. Yet traditional approaches to leadership development are woefully inadequate to meet their learning needs.

Fortunately, research and work done on both adult learning and on communities of practice offer solutions to this leadership development challenge. Two quite different approaches—one from working with the poor in Brazil, the second from working with global corporations—come together to mark a clear path.

The first is the pioneering work of Brazilian educator Paulo Freire. Working among the poorest of the poor in Brazil, Freire developed the practice and theory of *Critical Education.* He demonstrated that people who had never learned to read could quickly develop skills of literacy and complex reasoning if those skills would help them improve conditions within their communities. If they learned to think critically about the forces creating their poverty, they quickly learned the skills and analytic tools that could help relieve their condition.

Freire's work has since been substantiated by many others, in a wide variety of cultures and populations. The essential lesson is this: When people understand the forces creating the adverse conditions of their life and how they might change those forces, they become eager and rapid learners. They are capable of learning sophisticated skills that far surpass traditional assumptions about their intellectual capacity. And they learn these skills faster than anyone would have thought possible.

The second body of practice and research is that of communities of practice. This work has been pioneered in modern corporations, where training needs and efforts at knowledge management consume billions of dollars. Some core questions have been, How can people most quickly learn new skills? How is knowledge developed and shared within an organization? The concept community of practice was developed to illuminate that learning is a social experience. We humans learn best when in relationship with others who share a common practice. We self-organize as communities with those who have skills and knowledge that are important to us. Etienne Wenger, a pioneer in this field, states:

> Since the beginning of history, human beings have formed communities that accumulate collective learning into social practices—communities of practice. Tribes are an early example. More recent instances include the guilds of the Middle Ages that took on the stewardship of a trade, and scientific communities that collectively define what counts as valid knowledge in a specific area of investigation. Less obvious cases could be a local gardening club, nurses in a ward, a street gang, or a group of software engineers meeting regularly in the cafeteria to share tips.

Communities of practice demonstrate that it is natural for people to seek out those who have the knowledge and experience that they need. As people find others and exchange ideas, relationships develop and a community forms. This community becomes a rich marketplace where knowledge and experience are shared. It also becomes an incubator where new knowledge, skills, and competencies develop. In corporations, many of the core competencies (the core skills that are the organization's unique strengths) develop within these informal, self-organized communities, not from any intentional strategic or development strategy.

The literature on communities of practice is filled with stunning examples of how workers learn complex skills in rapid time when seated next to those who have the skill. And of how workers reach out electronically across the globe with a question to colleagues and receive back immediate, expert advice that resolves a crisis or dilemma.

These two very different fields—critical education and communities of practice—teach the same lessons. People learn very quickly when they have a need for the skills and information. If it will change their lives, if it will help them accomplish what is important to them, then everyone can become a good learner. We learn complex competencies and knowledge in a matter of weeks, not months or years. And people learn best in community, when they are engaged with one another, when everyone is both student and teacher, expert and apprentice, in a rich exchange of experiences and learnings.

Four Essential Activities for Supporting New Leaders

It is important that we figure out how to effectively support and nurture the pioneering new leaders that are appearing everywhere. And we need to find the means to develop large numbers of them. It is possible to accomplish quality support for many pioneering leaders if we work from a new unit of scale, that of leaders-in-community rather than leaders-as-individuals. This approach is based on the fact that we learn well in community, that learning accelerates and people quickly develop healthy and robust practices, new knowledge that works.

Four key types of support assist in developing leaders-in-community. Each of these four describes work for those organizations focused on supporting new leadership as the means to create sustainable change, such as foundations, non-governmental organizations, and governments.

Name, connect, nourish, illuminate

JOINED AS A COMMUNITY, LEADERS LEARN QUICKLY AND DEVELOP HEALTHY NEW PRACTICES.

BIRTH OF NEW SYSTEMS

Name the Community

Pioneering leaders act in isolation, unaware that they are part of a broader community. They act on intuition and experience, struggling to not revert to the practices of the past. They feel alone and strange, often criticized, even ridiculed, by their community. For believing that they can lead in new ways, solve entrenched problems, and create sustainable progress, they often get labeled negatively as idealists, dreamers, innocents.

Isolation dissolves when they learn that they are part of a community, that there are many more like them. They gain confidence and courage. They find new energy to stay in the challenges and struggles of pioneering.

The community they belong to is a community of practice, not of place, because it is formed among people who act from the same values and visions, and who are doing similar work. They may be a community of people working in education, or organic farming, or local government. They share the same type of work, yet their practices are varied and unique, specific to the needs of their local culture. In this way, the community is very diverse in its expression, and very united in its purpose.

Connect the Community

Once the community has been named, it is important that people find the means to connect with one another and to keep those connections strong and present. We live in a time when connecting across distance and difference has become much easier. Technology can facilitate working as community through dedicated Web sites, online conferences, and listserves. But technology is only a *supplement* to the need to be together in the same physical space from time to time. There is no substitute for being together, so periodic gatherings of the community, visits to each other's towns and worksites, and any other means to meet face-to-face are essential. The stronger the connections, the more support and new knowledge will be born from those connections.

Nourish the Community

Communities of practice need to be nourished with many different resources. They require ideas, methods, mentors, processes, information, technology, equipment, money. Each of these is important, but perhaps the greatest need is that of knowledge—knowing what techniques and processes work well. For example, a leader may be conducting a community development process yet know nothing of new means to engage the whole community, or new processes for valuing a community's assets. Without this knowledge, people either reinvent the wheel or use whatever process they know, even inappropriate or substandard ones.

To bring good resources to eager learners is such a simple and powerful means to promote the learning and practices of these pioneers. And these new leaders are already highly efficient users of resources—they've been stretching meager means for years.

Illuminate the Community

There is a critical need to tell the stories of these pioneering leaders-in-community, to get public attention for their efforts. Remember how difficult it is for any of us to see a new paradigm, even when it's right under our noses. People, if they do take notice, are most likely to see these new pioneers as inspiring but temporary deviations from the norm. It takes time, attention, and a consistent media focus for people to see them for what they are, examples of what's possible, of what our new world could look like. We need to hear their stories, celebrate their successes, and continue to support them as our beacons to the future.

Berkana's Experience with This Fourfold Approach

This approach emerged from the work of The Berkana Institute during the past several years. We didn't invent the model as much as we noticed that it was an accurate description of the work we found ourselves doing. For example, we'd been working with a global network of younger leaders, Pioneers of Change (www.pioneersofchange.net). Some of their members had participated in a Berkana initiative, "From the Four Directions," in which we support the creation of ongoing conversations among local leaders in many countries.

We had noted a trend among some of these younger pioneers: they were intent on establishing leadership learning centers in their own communities. They either were dreaming of how they might do this or were already engaged in creating an organized means to develop new leadership in their different nations. They were attending another meeting, unaware of the dreams they shared. Some later commented that they'd been hesitant to express their idea of a leadership center because it felt too strange. But when one younger woman convened a group to talk about her dream of building a learning village in Zimbabwe, her dream elicited the similar dreams of many others. Two staff from Berkana were present at that meeting and "named the community." Since that time in July 2001, Berkana and Pioneers of Change have partnered in supporting new leadership centers in Croatia, England, Holland, India, Senegal, and Zimbabwe. New centers continue to develop and are now supported by the Berkana Exchange.

Each of these centers is absolutely unique and engaged in very different activities to develop leadership in their communities and nations. Yet everyone benefits greatly from working as a community of practice, learning from one another, exchanging advice and information, and supporting one another with true friendship.

How Communities of Practice Differ from Networks

We live in a time when coalitions, alliances, and networks are growing. People have created many networks and, now, networks of networks. These networks are essential for successful change—they are the first step in people finding like-minded others. People usually network together for personal, even instrumental reasons. They move in and out of them based on how well they serve their own work. The formation of a network is an important, preliminary gathering step.

Communities of practice are the next step, and they are different in significant ways. They are *communities,* which means that people make a commitment to be available to each other, to offer support to share learning, to consciously develop new knowledge. They are there not only for their own needs, but for the needs of others. These communities succeed best when they start with some type of community formation process. People need to clarify their personal intent and commitment and, as a group, they need to agree on how they will work together, how they will support one another, and what their work will be (See Berkana's social processes for community formation at www. newworkspaces.net).

Also in a community of practice, the focus extends beyond the work of the community. There is an intentional commitment to advance the field of practice and to share those discoveries with anyone engaged in such work. For example, people working on developing local schools (because children in their Zimbabwean community can't afford school fees) find out how to do this by exchanging information and learning with other such initiatives anywhere on the planet. Through their work as a community of practice, not only do they get a schooling program going in Zimbabwe; the community of practice also makes its resources and knowledge available to anyone interested in such initiatives.

The speed with which people learn and grow in a community of practice is essential. Good ideas move rapidly among members, and from local to global. This new knowledge and wisdom are implemented quickly from exchanges among practitioners. The speed at which knowledge development and exchange happens is crucial, because the world needs this knowledge and wisdom *now*. Therefore, sponsoring communities of practice among pioneering leaders is a deliberate strategy to speed up the emergence of new leadership practices everywhere, to give the world the leadership it needs at this time.

Working with Life's Process for Global Change

The four stages of this process are based on an understanding of how change happens in all living systems. Life's process for change is termed *emergence*, and it is how local efforts achieve global impact. In nature, change never happens as a result of top-down, preconceived strategic plans or from the mandate of any single individual or boss. Change begins as local actions spring up simultane-ously around the system. If these changes remain disconnected, nothing hap-pens beyond each locale. However, when they become connected, local actions can emerge as a powerful influence at a more global or comprehensive level. (*Global* here means a larger scale, not necessarily the entire planet.)

These powerful *emergent phenomena* appear suddenly and surprisingly. Think about how the Berlin Wall suddenly came down, how the Soviet Union ended. In each case, there were many local actions, most of which were invisible and none of which was powerful enough to create big change. But when they joined together, new power emerged. What could not be accomplished by diplomacy, power politics, or protests suddenly happened. And each material-ized suddenly. Emergent phenomena always have these characteristics: They are much more powerful than the sum of their parts; they always possess capacities that are different from the local actions that engendered them; they always surprise us by their appearance.

Emergence is a process that is important to understand. It is the way life changes. However, it can result in good or ill. Emergence is seen in the growth of terrorism, street gangs, unhealthy organizational cultures. It all depends on the values and purpose used to organize local efforts.

Emergence only happens through connections. Therefore, any process that can catalyze connections becomes the means to achieve change at a global level. When we name, connect, nourish, and illuminate the work of local leaders, we are working intentionally with this powerful process. Through emergence, their small, local efforts can become a global force for change, powerful enough to create the world we all desire, where the human spirit is known as the blessing, not the problem.

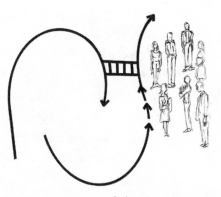

As old systems continue to fail, new systems are now available to welcome large numbers of people.

Note: The content of this article was based on long conversations and work with a number of colleagues, including Lotte Darso, Debbie Frieze, Manish Jain, Cire Kane, Marianne Knuth, Toke Moeller, Monica Nissan, Carole Schwinn, Bob Stilger, Tenneson Woolf, and the Berkana Wisdom Board.

Transforming Aggression into Creativity: An Ancient Practice for Solving Problems

with Geoff Crinean

Organizations today suffer from a severe disability when it comes to solving problems. In virtually every organization, regardless of mission and function, people are frustrated by problems that seem unsolvable. Every attempt to resolve a problem results in unintended consequences that dwarf the original one. Relationships worsen as people harden into opposing positions, each side insisting on its own solution, unwilling to consider alternatives. Too many problem-solving sessions become battlegrounds where decisions are made based on power rather than intelligence.

Consider the language used to describe problem solving. We "attack the problem," "tackle the issue," "take a stab at it," "wrestle it to the ground," "get on top of it." If colleagues argue with us, we complain that they "shot down my idea," "took pot shots at me," "used me for target practice," or that "I got killed." In the face of opposition, we "back down," "retreat," or "regroup." (Occasionally, we use gentler metaphors—we may "float an idea" or test it to see "if it has legs.") Such aggressive descriptions of problem solving point to a startling conclusion. We experience problem-solving sessions as war zones, we view competing ideas as enemies, and we use problems as weapons to blame and defeat opposition forces. No wonder we can't come up with real lasting solutions!

Aggressive problem-solving techniques manifest in subtle ways as well. Nearly every problem faced by an organization is exceedingly complex. Yet we act as if simple cause and effect is at work. We push to find the one simple reason things have gone wrong. We look for the one action, or the one person, that created this mess. As soon as we find someone to blame, we act as if we've solved the problem. Of course, it's always someone else's fault, never our own. This is the one real joy of scapegoating—we walk away and somebody else or their project takes the hit. Finding others to blame is the only reward of simplistic thinking.

But satisfaction in naming the scapegoat is momentary. Long-term, we've set in motion a number of disastrous unintended consequences that create an impotent and hostile organizational culture. In a culture of blame, people become protective and reactive, striking out in self-defense. Innovation and risk taking vanish. What increases are hardened positions, stronger factions, alliances, even cabals. Appreciation for diverse viewpoints disappears. People trust only those who think like they do. Real information goes underground, and angry gossip and paranoid rumors are all that circulate. Passive aggression appears in calculated strategies where people stonewall, delay, and sabotage. Thinking shrinks to moment-by-moment reactions and long-term strategic thinking disappears. Everybody seeks to protect themselves, and nobody thinks about the whole enterprise.

This sorry state of affairs is quite predictable. Aggression only breeds more aggression. It only creates more fear and anger. It is impossible to avoid this deteriorating cycle as long as aggressive tactics are pursued. *What has been less evident is that our approaches to problem solving are inherently aggressive.* We haven't noticed how our attempts to solve problems by seeking simplistic causes, by treating problems as enemies, by needing to assign blame, how all these behaviors are contributing to the increasing number of problems we face and the deterioration of an organization's or community's capacity to work to solve them.

There are healthy alternatives to this aggressive approach to problem solving. But before detailing a five-stage process, let's observe for a moment the sea of aggressive energy in which we currently swim.

An Aggressive Society

These days, our senses are bombarded with aggression. We are constantly confronted with global images of unending, escalating war and violence. In our personal lives, we encounter angry people cursing into cell phones, watch TV talk shows where guests and audiences intimidate each other verbally and sometimes physically, or attend public meetings that disintegrate into shouting matches. Aggression appears frequently in advertising images, from food products that promise to "hammer your hunger," to a recent candy commercial where formerly benign M&Ms became violent and beat up a noisy moviegoer to everyone else's satisfaction.

Aggression is not only the dominant energy of this time; we regard it as a positive attribute. Parents scream from the sidelines of their children's sports events: "Get aggressive!" Employees are rewarded for aggressive time lines and plans. Dictionaries define *aggressive* as describing hostile action but also positively as assertive, bold, and enterprising.

Aggression destroys relationships. People believe that in order to survive, they must combat the opposition. Fear and anger destroy hope for healthy communities, work groups, families, and organizations. Relationships fracture; distrust increases; people retreat into self-defense and isolation; paranoia becomes commonplace.

Aggression in Organizations

In many organizations, aggression is a nearly invisible medium that influences decisions and actions. It's evident in the consistent use of war and sports metaphors. We "bring in the big guns," "dominate the field," plan "a sneak attack," or "rally the troops." Recently, even e-mail has turned violent: "I'll shoot you an e-mail."

And organizational aggression is on the rise, mirroring the societal trend. Competition has become increasingly ruthless with strategies that aim to destroy competitors and achieve total market domination, rather than strategies of coexistence within well-defined niches. The resurgence of command-and-control leadership is a less obvious but strong form of aggression, where the will of one person is imposed on others with the demand for obedience and compliance.

Day to day, there's overt aggression in meetings where one or two people dominate, railroad the agenda, and insist on their opinion or strategy. Passive aggression is also common as people use delaying tactics, when they agree to do things and then fail to act, when they refuse to respond to communications or act contrary to prior agreements, when they act secretly and don't communicate what they're doing, when they resort to sarcasm and cutting humor.

Increasing aggression is having a profound impact on organizational relationships. Distrust is increasing, so much so that in one survey, managers reported that the primary reason they attend meetings is because they don't trust what their colleagues will do in their absence. More employees are retreating into self-protective stances, hoarding resources and information for fear of losing further control of their work. And worker stress levels are at an all-time high, as frequently reported in the popular press. It's now estimated that one-third of lost work days in Canada, England, and the United States are due to worker stress.

Until we find alternative means to work together without so much aggression, we will continue to experience increasing anger, frustration, impasse, and exhaustion.

Solving Problems Free from Aggression

For eons, humans have struggled to find less destructive ways of living together. Today, if we are to resolve the serious problems that afflict and impede us, we must find the means to work and live together with less aggression. The five-stage process described here originated from an ancient teaching in Tibet.

We have brought it forward, modified and expanded it, based on our experience of working in many large, complex organizations and communities who face intractable problems. This process allows individuals and groups to disengage from aggressive dynamics yet also to use the passion and energy of all involved to develop greater clarity and insight into truly creative solutions.

To step aside from aggressive responses to problem solving requires a little-used skill: *humility.* Humility is a brave act—we have to admit that we don't have the answer. We need more information, more insight. This kind of humility is rare in competitive, embattled organizations and communities, but it is what we need to find real solutions. One wise educator put it this way: "Humility is admitting that I don't know the whole story. Compassion is recognizing that you don't know it, either."

Hopefully, humility leads us out of our bunkers, to open ground where we step away from the rigidity of our positions and become a bit curious. We need to be open to the possibility that colleagues and even strangers have information and perspectives that may be of value to us. Only with their input do we stand a chance of seeing this problem in all its complexity. Every perspective, prejudice, and opinion offers more information. Our different positions allow us to see the situation more fully as soon as we realize that we're all on the same side—*that the problem is the problem.*

Five Stages to Solving Complex Problems

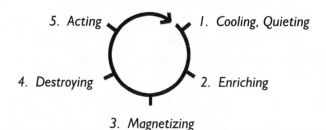

5. Acting   1. Cooling, Quieting

4. Destroying   2. Enriching

3. Magnetizing

In order to develop a full understanding of a complex problem and to know what to do to resolve it, there are five precise activities to complete in sequence:

1. Cooling, Quieting
2. Enriching through Fruitful Opposition
3. Magnetizing Resources
4. Precise Destroying
5. Intelligent Action

These five stages are depicted here as a cycle because they work developmentally, one stage creating the conditions for the next. This developmental sequence, however, can sometimes be gone through very quickly, or a group might spend a great deal of time in one stage and move rapidly through the next. Each stage has a form associated with it, a shape that provides the appropriate structure for the work at hand. Also, there are different core behaviors that facilitate the inquiry for each stage.

Stage One: Cooling, Quieting
Imagine your most recent experience in a conflicted situation. Most likely, people were arguing their position, not listening, raising their voices, acting out, doing power plays—in essence, acting aggressively. Nothing positive ever results from this escalating conflict, yet we're stuck in the drama. Now imagine what might have been possible if someone had intervened with a process to lessen the drama, to cool down the situation. This first stage does just that, by using an ancient, pacifying form, the circle.

The circle is the shape that cools, quiets, pacifies (makes peaceful). It is the form of equality, the most common and enduring form of human meeting. Circles have been found from about half a million years ago as early human ancestors sat around fires, trying to get warm. The equality of the circle was important even then. Had they sat in a rectangle or any other form, some of them would have frozen!

To pacify a highly conflicted group, you have to move into a circle (or a number of small circles). As soon as you sit in this form and it becomes clear that everyone will have a chance to speak, things quiet down. Anyone who persists in being dramatic or loud in a circle soon looks like a fool. Circles create soothing space, where even reticent people can realize that their voice is welcome. As the drama drains, people still will speak passionately, but with a quieter intensity.

The process is quite straightforward. Start with a question that focuses on people's personal experience with the issue. Why is this issue important to you? How does this issue impact your work or life? What's been your experience in trying to resolve this dilemma?

You ask the question and then go around the circle inviting everyone to speak, in turn, and within a limited time period. People who choose not to speak may pass and contribute later if they like. As each person speaks, everyone else is silent, listening as best they can. People may ask questions if they don't understand something being said, but this is not the time for exchanges or debates. The task is to have each voice heard, for each person to make a contribution to the circle. (See www.turningoneanother.net for different processes of using circles with large and small groups.)

Cooling, Quieting
Curiosity and Patience

This process of listening offers many benefits. The first is that good listeners are created as people feel listened to. Listening is a reciprocal process—we become more attentive to others if they have attended to us. We are often surprised when people truly listen to us. Their unexpected acceptance encourages us to listen better.

The second benefit is that listening brings people together. You can see this happening physically in a circle. As people quiet down and get more engaged, they lean in. The circle becomes tighter. The room gets quieter, the volume decreases substantially, yet the intensity of listening is palpable.

And as we listen, we develop greater awareness that each of us is human, struggling with life's challenges. We may never agree on an issue or share the same values, but as soon as we realize there's a person behind the position, we become more open to them, less reactive.

The purpose of first quieting, calming, and pacifying is to develop a richer appreciation of the complexity of the problem, using a process that begins to bring people together. Every person has a somewhat different perspective, by virtue of individual differences and also because we each live in a different part of the organization or community. The world doesn't look exactly the same to any two people, and a circle provides the form to gather many different perspectives without as much judgment or defensiveness.

The core behaviors of this first process are patience and curiosity. We have to be willing to give up our soapboxes and become curious about other perspectives. And we have to be patient—it takes time to go around a circle and give everyone equal time. If we become impatient, it's an indication that we're still holding on to our position. We just want to get this over with so we can win using more aggressive approaches. But, usually, what's being said by others begins to awaken our curiosity. We learn things we didn't know and develop more awareness of how other people are affected by the problem under consideration.

Stage Two: Enriching through Fruitful Opposition

After the initial process of cooling and quieting, it's essential to return to the source of the conflict, which is people's different perspectives and positions. In order to understand a problem in its complexity, we have to learn much more about it. We achieve this understanding by giving each person or position ample opportunity to explain their reasoning in depth. What's required here is *to amplify the differences* as the means to create a fuller, detailed appreciation of the situation or problem. We are seeking to enrich our understanding from the realization that no one person or position has a sufficient picture of what's going on.

To create this differentiation and depth, it helps to sit around a square table, to literally "take sides." People need to choose which side they're on. (More than four sides is fine, as long as it doesn't go beyond an octagon. And people can switch sides as the process evolves.) You can also do this seated as an audience, with each side presenting from the front. The fact that most public forums use such a form explains why they only increase conflict and entrenched positions. They begin by amplifying differences, rather then quieting and calming the situation. If you begin with taking sides, it's guaranteed that you will only exacerbate the conflict.

Enriching through Fruitful Opposition
Respect and Clear Thinking

Each side is responsible for developing its position in depth. This is not the time for sloganeering or campaigning. The task is to go deeply into the rationale and logic of each position. It is important to keep the exploration of each side distinct—we are not seeking compromise, blending of views, consensus, or negotiation. Each position has its own logic, and the goal is to develop the unique integrity of each side.

Respect and clear thinking are the core behaviors of this stage. We listen attentively, even to those with whom we profoundly disagree. Such respect is easier now that people have sat in circle together and developed more rapport and patience. Respect also means that we're open to the possibility that we'll hear something useful from our opponents. We are willing to acknowledge that others have insight and wisdom that are useful to the group.

Clear thinking is essential. We move away from emotions (no matter how much we care about the issue) and instead use reason to develop greater clarity about what's going on. We want to clear away the fog created by our emotional investment in the issue. As each side presents its analysis of the problem, others simply listen. After a while, the inherent complexity of the situation becomes quite evident. Often, people are overwhelmed as they realize just how complex things really are. But this inundation is of great benefit, because it moves people off of their certainty platforms. Confused and overwhelmed, we become open to new interpretations and possibilities. Thus, confusion is the necessary precursor for letting go of entrenched positions and moving into creative exploration together.

At the end of this stage of differentiation and taking sides, notice that people begin to move out of the square or audience form and begin to cluster in messier ways because they want to talk with each other. One paradoxical consequence of exploring differences is that groups emerge at the other end feeling somewhat unified. The boundaries of the different positions have lost their hardness, and people begin to talk together as one cohesive group, wanting to resolve the problem together. This feeling of cohesiveness is an essential prerequisite for Stage Three, when it will be an important means to attract needed resources

Stage Three: Magnetizing Resources

In magnetism, only opposites attract. Two magnets will repel each other if the same poles (or energy charge) are brought together. Yet when opposing magnetic poles are brought near each other, they snap together in a strong embrace. The same principle of attraction and rejection is relevant to this stage of problem solving.

After progressing through the stages of cooling and enriching, it is common for people to feel good about working together as a group, to be humbled by the complexity of the issue, and to be energized to move forward in finding a solution. It's a complex array of predictable emotions. People will be both tired and motivated, confused yet confident. However, it's also common for people at this stage to want to launch into action planning. Taking action relieves us of the oppressive feelings of confusion and overwhelm. We are eager to do anything rather than linger longer in these uncomfortable states.

However, if actions are determined at this stage, generally they will be the wrong ones. We do not yet have a sufficient understanding of the issue's complexity to know what actions will be useful. If we rush into actions prematurely, we run the risk of setting in motion a long chain of unintended consequences. Stage Three takes us deeper into the issue, rather than encouraging us to leap prematurely onto the stage of action.

The form that characterizes the work of Stage Three is a half circle, a very inviting yet humbling symbol. It indicates that however far we've come in our understanding of the problem, *we're only halfway there*. Our comprehension of what's going on is still incomplete, and we need more perspectives and information to complete the circle of understanding.

As a result of working well through the first two processes, people approach this stage with more confidence. They have worked well enough together to believe that they can find the resources, information and support they need. And it's true that groups at this stage do attract what they need, different and opposing points of view.

Generosity is also a core behavior of this stage. We're no longer working in a reactive, self-protective mode. We've developed stronger relationships with colleagues and have increased our understanding. As our curiosity has grown, as we've moved out of our bunkers, it becomes easier to feel open and welcoming. Humbled that we know only half of what we need to know, it's easier to feel generous, welcoming new viewpoints and uncomfortable information.

To complete the circle of understanding, it is very helpful to sit arrayed along the curve of a half-circle, facing out to the blank, uncompleted circle. There's something unusual about sitting in this form, staring into a blank space. You can put up flip charts or a white board in the empty half of the circle, but it's important to keep people focused on the blank space, not on each other. You can also draw a circle on paper that is split down the middle. Fill in one side with a summary of your understanding. Leave the other side blank, to be filled in during this process.

A variety of questions help fill in the blanks:

— Who else needs to be here?

— What are we blind to? What can't we yet see?

— What additional information and perspectives do we need?

Magnetizing Resources
Generosity and Patience

In answering these questions, the group is creating its next piece of work. Whoever is identified as missing has to be invited into the group. Whatever information is lacking has to be researched and brought in for deliberation. Time is required to go find the people, ideas, and resources that have been identified. It is important for the group to set a realistic but efficient timeline for this work.

Our willingness to acknowledge that we need other perspectives and experiences makes us more attractive to others. The more sincerely we acknowledge our need for their different views and insights, the more they will be magnetized to join us. As our humility and openness becomes evident, and as our generosity grows, word gets out that we're a good group to work with. This reputation also helps attract the people that we need to complete our circle of understanding.

Stage Four: Precise Destroying
Although we live in an aggressive culture, people often recoil from the word *destroying*. Yet if we look honestly at what's going on in organizations, destroy-

ing is the most common response to problems. And *it's the first response*, rather than being the last action after careful consideration of the situation. Too many organizations use weapons of mass destruction rather than smart bombs. These WMDs include sweeping budget cuts, where everything is reduced, rather than intelligent decisions to cut back in specific areas. Or massive lay-offs. Or constant reorganizations that obliterate the most recent reorganization. We don't seem to know how to act with precision; instead we routinely resort to carpet bombing.

Destroying is a necessary function in life. Everything has its season, and all things eventually lose their effectiveness and die. We do as much harm holding onto programs and people beyond their natural life span as we do when we employ massive organizational air strikes. However, destroying comes at the end of life's cycle, not as a first response. Hence it is Stage Four here, coming after deep, thoughtful analysis by a group that is thinking well together. At this stage, *precision destroying is necessary to create more capacity for the work going forward.* We can see now what precise elements of the situation are impeding movement forward, what specific things need to be let go of because they are no longer necessary or appropriate for the work we must do.

Many different things need to be considered for destruction: outmoded beliefs; inappropriate or harmful values; traditional practices that no longer make sense; habitual behaviors that are dysfunctional; aspects of the culture that impede future direction; programs that have outlived their usefulness; policies that don't work as intended; specific individuals who refuse to change or who block progress.

At this stage in the problem-solving process, we can be trusted to act with precision and discipline. We no longer react defensively, intent on getting rid of people and things that threaten us. We have a very clear picture of the problem and are able to use this new found clarity to exercise real discernment. We act as intelligent and insightful contributors rather than as excluded or embattled members of the organization or community. We now are skilled enough to discern those focused acts of destroying that will yield real benefit.

The form for Precision Destroying is the triangle. A triangle is a very stable structure, sitting on a broad base that supports its apex. The group can sit as a triangle, leaving the apex area open, with a flip chart or small white board occupying that narrow point. Or people can draw a triangle and focus on the apex area. The core skills of this stage are discipline and discernment. We are restricted by the triangle to nominate only a small number of things to be destroyed in that narrow apex. We apply laserlike discernment to a very complex situation.

Precise Destroying
Discipline and Discernment

Precision destroying is naturally compassionate. We no longer act from self-defense, striking out at what we think harms us. We're clear about which things impede solutions, which small elements hold us back or burden us with the past. When we determine what to destroy, we do so from a profound appreciation of the problem. We do not act from fear or anger, but from clarity and compassion.

Stage Five: Intelligent Action

This last stage is the harvest for working through the first four. We are now a cohesive, smart group of people who have developed genuine perspective and depth about the problem under consideration. We have become good systems thinkers because we've included so many diverse and contrasting views and information in our analysis. We can't help but appreciate the dense interconnections and multiple dynamics at play in this situation. We've also developed very useful skills in working well together. We've become better listeners, become more open and curious, developed new thinking and analytic skills. We've also learned to work with people we had misunderstood, ignored, or feared. We've become a more intelligent, diverse, inclusive, and confident team, ready to go to work. The core behaviors of this stage are commitment and teamwork. We don't have to create them or go off to be trained; they are the result of all the work we've done to get this far.

The form for this stage is the existing organization. Now is the time to use the processes that people are familiar with: action planning, strategy setting, project planning, budgeting, measurement. These processes have an important role to play. What's been missing from them in the past is good thinking about how best to apply them. Bored or exhausted, people have used them in rote fashion without insight or intelligence. Or they have been forced to use them in all situations, even those that make no sense. However, now these well-worn and tired processes can be infused with the light of clear thinking and the energy of strong commitment. Newly developed insights can be used to determine intelligently which actions, measures, and strategies make the most sense. Empowerment will occur naturally, as people proceed to change and discard existing processes and methods that are dysfunctional or nonsensical.

Intelligent Action
Commitment, Teamwork, and Learning

It's important to note that leaders need to be prepared for big change. Once any group has developed this level of insight and rapport, they cannot be pushed back into small boxes or compliant behavior. With their intelligence awakened, people want to contribute, want to change things, want to make things happen. They will work with existing structures and processes, but they will be altering and adapting them as needed, almost without noticing. Too often, leaders fear a loss of control and attempt to rein in such groups. Their own fear pushes them back into aggressive patterns of command and control. However, the smart leader understands the level of accomplishment attained by this group and the depth of understanding now available. It is time to celebrate the fact that so much commitment and intelligence are now in active use in the organization.

When we can lay down our fear and anger and choose responses other than aggression, we create the conditions for bringing out the best in us humans. Without aggression, it becomes possible to think well, to be curious about differences, and to enjoy each other's company. Our energy finds new channels in creativity rather than defense. We learn that it is possible to feel passionate about a position without having to resist or outmaneuver those with differing passions.

As we strive to make our organizations and communities work decently in these difficult times, if we are to find true solutions to the problems that afflict us, it is essential that we understand the price we pay for our aggressive methods. If we are to work together more intelligently, we will need to choose processes that evoke our curiosity, humility, generosity, and wisdom. The ultimate benefit is that we learn that it is good, once again, to work together.

Seven Hundred Years to Go

The Dalai Lama told a group of my colleagues not to be anxious.
The work we're doing now, he said, will bear fruit in seven hundred years.

We awake in a brave new world and we don't
know what we did. For years, images in our
periphery hovered, haunting, compelling us be brave.
We turned to embrace them and they vanished with our effort.
By this pursuit, we bred our own exhaustion.

Hope wedded us to loss. Lost words,
lost colleagues, lost clarity. In loss we
cowered, sometimes together, often alone,
in the dark cave where the future shadowed us,
history at our back, promise
glimmering at the entrance.

And now the future is streaming through the walls,
consuming our faint fires, beckoning us move outside
to this bright geography so obviously real.
Now it is the present calling, not
the future, and we are hovering at the entrance,
blinded by this sudden illumination.

After years of living with immobilized
imagination, this present is perplexing.
Strange now to be sought by a
world we had been seeking, to be greeted by
companions after so much time alone,
to have arrived and now feel lost.
Why is this new world suddenly here?
Was it our great efforting, our
careful, crafted work, our
small acts of cautious daring that
brought us here? Yes.

No. It was changing all the time anyway.

We were faithful dwellers, dreamers.
Through a glass, darkly we
drew images in the dim smoky light.
We saw shimmers on the wall and
claimed them—vague, strange,
ours.

But they were never ours.
The future was drawing us.

It was changing all the time, anyway.

Personal
Attending to Our Footsteps

Living Our Interconnectedness
Willing to Be Disturbed
Reclaiming Time to Think
Listening
Raising Our Children
Ending Our Silence
Everything Has a Deep Dream

Here you will find several short essays, each of which challenges you to notice how your behavior is being affected by these times. We need to notice how we're being influenced by the more negative trends of society, such things as speed, polarization, ceaseless activity, and no time for reflection. We also need to notice whether we're responding with courage or silence. And we very much need to pay attention to what's happening to our children and how this culture is influencing them.

Choose Life, only that and always, and at whatever risk. To let life leak out, to let it wear away by the mere passage of time, to withhold giving it and spreading it is to choose nothing.

—Sr. Ann Kelly

Living Our Interconnectedness

The dense and tangled web of life—the interconnected nature of reality—now reveals itself on a daily basis. In recent years, think about how much you've learned about people, nations, and ways of life that previously you'd known nothing about. We've been learning how the lives of those far away affect our own and how we affect theirs. We're beginning to realize that to live peacefully together on this planet, we need to be in new relationships, especially with those far distant from us.

When my children were small, I had a refrigerator magnet that read, "If mama ain't happy, ain't nobody happy." Perhaps that was my children's first lesson in systems thinking. We adults are learning this, too. If others don't feel safe, we aren't safe. If others are struggling, we experience the consequence of their struggle. If others are poor, no matter how wealthy we are, we experience the consequences of their impoverishment.

Many great teachers have been trying to teach us this for thousands of years. Buddhism teaches that any one thing is here because of everything else. Jesus said that if "ye are not one, ye are not mine." Chief Seattle reminded us that "the earth does not belong to us; we belong to the earth." And the American naturalist, John Muir, commented that when we tug on any one part of the web of life, we get the whole web. But in spite of such timeless and ancient wisdom, we've turned a deaf ear on all these wise ones.

Why are we so resistant to acknowledging our interdependence and interconnectedness? I recall years ago sitting at a conference table in Washington, D.C., where we were discussing how to create resilient communities in the face of Y2K. I enthusiastically said that people were going to learn about all the webs of interconnections that make our lives work. A noted physicist leaned across the table, looked me in the eye, and uttered this wisdom: "Meg, people don't want to know they're interconnected."

Since then, I've had people prove him right many times over. Acknowledging that we're responsible for more than ourselves, that our work and lives affect many others—this is just too painful. Nobody wants to take on more responsibility, especially at this time when so many of us feel overworked and overwhelmed. Yet if we don't wake up to how intensely we're connected, we'll continue to create more harm through our blind, self-serving actions.

And if we've grown up in Western culture, interconnectedness denies the major organizing premise we've been taught. In the West, people have spent many decades drawing lines and boxes around interconnected phenomena. The world has been chunked into pieces rather than recognized for its webby nature. Think of how many lines and boundaries exist: org charts, job descriptions, town boundaries, nation states, ethnic identities. All these neat lines obscure the natural messiness of this interconnected world.

Whenever people become fearful, the boundaries become fortress walls behind which we seek protection. People are rallied to war by reinforcing the lines of national or ethnic identity. At work, in times of uncertainty, the lines also grow stronger. Roles become more delineated, and individuals get measured for their singular work, even though every job and problem is connected to many others. As the organization asserts more control, people withdraw and disengage. They just do what they're told. By failing to notice that we're all in this together, organizations breed new levels of incapacity.

I had a stunning experience with this self-protective work attitude shortly after the first anthrax incident in 2001 occurred in Palm Beach, Florida. A friend of mine is a judge at the Palm Beach courthouse. Her secretary noticed that someone had been at her desk—papers were disturbed, things moved around. Given the danger from anthrax and other possible security threats, the judge immediately called building security. I watched as the security guard blandly told her that it was not his job to secure the secretary's office. "My job is to secure the judge's chambers, that's all." He could not be convinced otherwise, even in the presence of an airborne poison. He knew his box and refused to think about this new world where danger knows no boundaries.

But I do not fault this security guard. He, like so many, had learned to keep his head down, to not make waves, to do what you're told. He took protection in his job description—he was just doing his job. Too many organizations, as they maintain control by managing by the boxes, have created millions of withdrawn, dependent, frightened, and cynical employees. Exactly what we don't need if we're to survive this uncertain time.

Our safety and future depend on each of us stepping outside the lines and participating intelligently in this complex world of interconnections. Here are two hard truths about living and working in an interconnected system that might call us out of our boxes. And that might help leaders define the work that needs to be done.

– *In an interconnected system, there is no such thing as simple cause and effect.* There's no one person to blame or to take the credit. We have yet to learn this. Watch how, in any crisis or success, people immediately assign blame or take all the credit. Why has crime decreased over the past few years? Police say its more police; judges say it's due to tougher sentences; parents say it's better parenting; teachers, economists, social workers, elected officials—everyone believes it's because of their singular contribution. No one wants to share the truth that it was everyone's contribution, interacting in inexplicable ways, that gave birth to the success.

– *Focusing only makes things fuzzier.* The more we study a complex phenomenon, the more confused we are bound to become. Few people like to feel confused or to be confronted by messiness. But interrelated phenomena—life—are very messy. The longer we study a system, the more complex it becomes. This is incredibly frustrating. Our attempts at understanding (reading the reports, listening to different commentaries, thinking about the issue) only serve to drag us into further complexity. Instead of clarity, we experience more uncertainty. What gave rise to modern terrorism? How do we create cleaner air? What leads to smarter students? Safer communities?

Seeing the System

Since our very survival depends on our becoming better systems thinkers, we need to learn to see the systems we're participating in. If not, we'll never resolve these questions: How can we act intelligently when things are fuzzy? Where do we intervene to change something when we can't determine straightforward cause and effect? What kinds of actions make sense when we're confronted with increasing uncertainty?

Here are a few means for being able to see a system and its webs of connections:

— *Start something and see who notices it.* It's only after we initiate something in a system that we see the threads that connect. Usually, someone we don't even know suddenly appears, either outraged or helpful. We didn't know there was any connection between us, but their response makes the connection clear. Now that they've identified themselves, we need to develop a relationship with them.

— *Whatever you initiate, expect unintended consequences.* Every effort to change a system creates these, because we can't see the interactions ahead of time. One very visible example of unintended consequences is what happens every time humans try to change the natural ecology of a place. Fertilizer is introduced to farm fields without noticing how rain water connects fields to oceans. Over time, we've got bountiful crops but fewer fish. I know one think tank that created a "Museum of Unintended Consequences." They wanted to notice all the impacts of any societal change effort. When we're willing to look at unintended consequences, they teach a great deal about how a system operates.

— *Reflect, often.* The system reveals itself to us all the time. The problem is we seldom stop to notice what just happened. Without such reflection, we go blindly on our way, ignoring the learnings, creating more unintended consequences, and failing to achieve anything useful. It's amazing to me how much we *do*, but how little time we spend reflecting on what we just did.

— *Seek out different interpretations.* Run ideas by many different people, to see things through their unique perceptions. Everyone in a complex system has, at minimum, a slightly different interpretation. The more interpretations we gather, the easier it is to gain a sense of the whole.

— *Look for insights to emerge out of messiness.* Puzzling and messy situations often lead us to simplistic and stupid behaviors. Either we grab onto an easy answer, or we decide to take actions that have no clear rational. But confusion can create the condition for intuitions and insights to appear, often when we least expect them. If they appear, they usually can be trusted. In fact, it's common for many people to arrive at the same conclusion at the same time. In the Quaker tradition, this is called "a gathered meeting." It's far better than struggling for false consensus.

These processes work well to bring an interconnected system into focus. We're then capable of making more intelligent decisions that respond to the complexity rather than trying to deny it. These processes also foster inclusion, so they create much improved relationships between colleagues and neighbors from different parts of the system.

I'd like us to start proving the physicist wrong and accept the fact that we live in an interconnected world. It takes courage to face this fact, yet it's the only way the world will change for the better.

Willing to Be Disturbed

Most people I meet want to develop more harmonious and satisfying relation-ships—in their organizations, communities, and personal lives. But we may not realize that this desire can only be satisfied by partnering with new and strange allies: uncertainty and confusion. Most of us weren't trained to like confusion or to admit when we feel hesitant and uncertain.

In schools and organizations, value is placed on sounding assured and confident. People are rewarded for stating opinions as if they're facts. Quick answers abound; pensive questions have disappeared from most organizations. Confusion has yet to appear as a higher-order value or as a behavior that organizations eagerly reward.

And as life continues speeding up (adding to our confusion), we don't have time to be uncertain. We don't have time to listen to anyone who expresses a new or different position. In meetings and in the media, often we listen to others just long enough to determine whether we agree with them or not. We rush from opinion to opinion, listening for those tidbits and sound bites that confirm our position. Gradually we become more certain but less informed.

We can't continue on this path if we want to find approaches and solutions to the problems that plague us. The world now is quite perplexing. We no longer live in those lovely days when life felt predictable, when we actually knew what to do next. In this increasingly complex world, it's impossible to see what's going on. The only way to see more of the complexity is to ask many others for their perspectives and experiences. Yet if we open ourselves to their differing perceptions, then we will find ourselves inhabiting the uncomfortable space of not knowing.

It is very difficult to give up certainty—these positions, beliefs, explanations define us and lie at the core of our personal identity. Certainty is a lens to interpret what's going on, and, as long as our explanations work, we feel a sense of stability and security. But in a changing world, certainty doesn't give us stability; it actually creates more chaos. As we stay locked in our position and refuse to adapt and change, the things we hoped would stay together fall apart. It's a traditional paradox expressed in many spiritual traditions: By holding on, we destroy what we hope to preserve; by letting go, we feel secure in accepting what is.

I believe that this changing world requires much less certainty and far more curiosity. I'm not suggesting we let go of our beliefs, only that we become curious about what someone else believes. As we open ourselves to the disturbing differences, sometimes we discover that another's way of interpreting the world actually is essential to our survival.

The global system we inhabit is dense and tangled. We each live in a different part of this complexity. And, no two people are identical. Therefore, it's impossible for two people to see things exactly the same. You can test this out for yourself. Take any event that you've shared with others (a speech, a movie, a current event, a major problem), and ask your colleagues and friends to describe their interpretation of that event. I think you'll be amazed at how many different explanations you'll hear. You'll end up with a rich tapestry of interpretations much more interesting than your single one.

I find that the first step to becoming curious is to admit that I'm not succeeding in figuring things out alone. If my solutions don't work as well as I'd like, if my explanations of why something happened don't feel sufficient, I take these as signs that it's time to begin asking others about what they see and think. I try to move past the lazy and superficial conversations where I pretend to agree with someone else rather than inquire seriously into their perspective. I try and become a conscious listener, actively listening for differences.

There are many ways to sit and listen for the differences. Lately, I've been listening for what surprises me. What did I just hear that startled me? This isn't easy—I'm accustomed to sit there nodding my head as someone voices what I agree with. But when I notice what surprises me, I'm able to see my own views more clearly, including my beliefs and assumptions.

Noticing what surprises and disturbs me has been a very useful way to see invisible beliefs. If what you say surprises me, I must have been assuming something else was true. If what you say disturbs me, I must believe something contrary to you. My shock at your position exposes my own position. When I hear myself saying, "How could anyone believe something like that?" a light comes on for me to see my own beliefs. These moments are great gifts. If I can see my beliefs and assumptions, I can decide whether I still value them.

If you're willing to be disturbed, I recommend that you begin a conversation with someone who thinks differently than you do. Listen as best you can for what's different, for what surprises you. Try to stop the voice of judgment or opinion. Just listen. At the end of this practice, notice whether you learned anything new. Notice whether you developed a better relationship with the person you just talked with. If you try this with several people, you might find yourself laughing in delight as you realize how many unique ways there are to be human.

We have the opportunity many times a day, every day, to be the one who listens to others, curious rather than certain. And the greatest benefit that comes to those who listen is that we develop closer relationships with those we thought we couldn't understand. When we listen with less judgment, we always develop better relationships with each other. It's not differences that divide us. It's our judgments that do. Curiosity and good listening bring us back together.

Sometimes we hesitate to listen for differences because we don't want to change. We're comfortable with our lives, and if we listened to anyone who raised questions, we'd have to get engaged in changing things. If we don't listen, things can stay as they are. But most of us do see things in our life or in the world that we would like to be different. If that's true, we have to listen more, not less. And we have to be willing to move into the discomfort of uncertainty and confusion.

We can't be creative if we refuse to be confused. Change always starts with confusion; cherished interpretations must dissolve to make way for the new. Of course, it's scary to give up what we know, but the abyss is where newness lives. When we're bold enough to we move through the fear and enter the abyss, we rediscover we're creative.

As the world grows more strange, perplexing, and difficult, I don't believe most of us want to keep struggling through it alone. I can't know what to do from my own narrow perspective. I know I need a better understanding of what's going on. I want to sit down with you and talk about all the frightening and hopeful things I observe, and listen to what frightens you and gives you hope. I need new ideas and solutions for the problems I care about. I know I need to talk to you to discover those. I need to learn to value your perspective, and I want you to value mine. I expect to be disturbed, even jarred, by what I hear from you. I expect to feel confused and displaced—my world won't feel as stable or familiar to me once we talk.

One last thing. As I explore my willingness to be disturbed, I'm learning that we don't have to agree with each other in order to think well together. There is no need for us to be joined at the head. We are joined already by our human hearts.

Reclaiming Time to Think

We humans possess some unique capacities. We can stand apart from what's going on, think about it, question it, imagine it being different. We are also curious. We want to know "Why?" We figure out "How?" We think about what's past; we dream forward to the future. We create what we want rather than just accept what is. So far, we're the only species we know that does this.

As the world speeds up, we're forfeiting these wonderful human capacities. Do you have as much time to think as you did a year ago? When was the last time you spent time reflecting on something important to you? At work, do you have more or less time now to think about what you're doing? Are you encouraged to spend time thinking with colleagues and coworkers?

In this speed culture, we now equate productivity with speed. If it can be done faster, we assume it's more productive. A recent trend in some companies is to hold meetings standing up. These meetings (or perhaps they should be called "football huddles"), are touted as more productive, but the only measure used is that they take less time. If people are kept standing, the meeting ends sooner. No one measures the productivity of these meetings by asking whether people have developed wiser solutions, better ideas, or more trusting relationships.

If we can pause for a moment and see what we are losing in this speed-up, I can't imagine that we would continue with this bargain. We're giving up the very things that make us human. Our road to hell is being paved with hasty intentions. I hope we can notice what we're losing—in our day-to-day lives, in our community, in our world. I hope we'll be brave enough to slow things down.

But I don't believe anybody is going to give us time to think. We have to reclaim it for ourselves.

Thinking is the place where intelligent actions begin. We pause long enough to look more carefully at a situation, to see more of its character, to think about why it's happening, to notice how it's affecting us and others. Paulo Freire used critical thinking as a nonviolent approach to revolutionary change. First in Brazil, and then in many poor communities around the world, he taught poor people how to think about their lives and the forces that were impoverishing them. Nobody believed that exhausted and struggling poor people could become intelligent thinkers. But it is easy for people to develop this capacity when they see how thinking can change their lives and the lives of those they love.

Our lives are not as desperate as those poor, and we may not notice that we're losing the possibility of a fully human life. To see whether you're losing anything of value to yourself, here are some questions to ask yourself: Are my relationships with those I love improving or deteriorating? Is my curiosity about the world increasing or decreasing? What things anger me today as compared to a few years ago? Which of my behaviors do I value, and which do I dislike? Generally, am I feeling more peaceful or more stressed? Am I becoming someone I respect?

If answering those questions helps you notice anything in your life that you'd like to change, you will need time to think about it. But don't expect anybody to give you this time. You will have to claim it for yourself.

No one will give it to you because thinking is always dangerous to the status quo. Those benefiting from the present system have no interest in your new ideas. In fact, your thinking is a threat to them. The moment you start thinking, you'll want to change something. You'll disturb the current situation. We can't expect those few who are well-served by the current reality to give us time to think. If we want anything to change, we are the ones who have to reclaim time to think.

In U.S. culture, thinking is not highly prized. In our frenzy to make things happen, to take action, we've devalued thinking and view it as an impediment to action. We've created a strange dualism between thinking and acting, I find this dualism to be very artificial and problematic.

In my experience, when something is important to us, there's no distance between thinking and acting. We are engaged with the issue (thinking), and we take action (doing). In group after group, I've watched people look thoughtfully at a situation and gain some understanding of its dynamics or its potential. After that experience, they can't help themselves. They step into action. It doesn't matter what culture it is, whenever people develop ideas that can change their lives, they act. People don't sit around figuring out the risks or waiting until someone else develops an implementation strategy. They just start. If an action doesn't work, they try something different.

Inside any bureaucracy, there's a huge gap between ideas and actions, what's known these days as a problem with "execution." But this failure to implement doesn't come from a thinking/doing division. It's the result of people not caring about the work. They didn't develop the project, they know it won't change anything, and nobody takes risks for something they don't believe in. But when it's our idea, a result of our thinking together, and we see how it might truly benefit our lives, then we act immediately on any promising notion. And we keep at it until we discover a real solution.

Taking time to think about those things that might truly change our lives always provides us with other gifts. Determination, energy, and courage appear spontaneously when we care deeply about something. We take risks that are unimaginable in any other context. Here's how Bernice Johnson Reagon, a gifted singer and songwriter, describes her own and others fearless acts during the civil rights movement:

Now I sit back and look at some of the things we did, and I say, "What in the world came over us?" But death had nothing to do with what we were doing. If somebody shot us, we would be dead. And when people died, we cried and went to funerals. And we went and did the next thing the next day, because it was really beyond life and death. It was really like sometimes you know what you're supposed to be doing. And when you know what you're supposed to be doing, it's somebody else's job to kill you.

While we may not be facing a life-and-death decision, we may be dying a slow death. If we feel we're changing in ways we don't like, or seeing things in the world that need to be different, then we need time to think about this. We need time to think about what we might do and where we might start to change things. We need time to develop clarity and courage. If we want our world to be different, our first act needs to be reclaiming time to think. Nothing will change for the better until we do that.

Listening

Listening is such a simple act. It requires us to be present, and that takes prac-
tice, but we don't have to do anything else. We don't have to advise, or coach,
or sound wise. We just have to be willing to sit there and listen. If we can do
that, we create moments in which real healing is available.

I have seen the healing power of good listening so often that I wonder if you've
noticed it also. There may have been a time when a friend was telling you such
a painful story that you became speechless. You couldn't think of anything to
say, so you just sat there, listening closely, but not saying a word. And what was
the result of your heartfelt silence, of your listening?

A young black South African woman taught some of my friends a profound
lesson about listening. She was sitting in a circle of women from many nations,
and each woman had the chance to tell a story from her life. When her turn
came, she began quietly to tell a story of true horror—of how she had found
her grandparents slaughtered in their village. Many of the women were West-
erners, and in the presence of such pain, they instinctively wanted to do something. They wanted to fix, to make it better, anything to remove the pain of this
tragedy from such a young life. The young woman felt their compassion but
also felt them closing in. She put her hands up, as if to push back their desire to
help. She said, "I don't need you to fix me. I just need you to listen to me."

She taught many women that day that being listened to is enough. If we can
speak our story and know that others hear it, we are somehow healed by that.
During the Truth and Reconciliation Commission hearings in South Africa, many
of those who testified to the atrocities they had endured under apartheid would
speak of being healed by their own testimony. They knew that many people
were listening to their story. One young man who had been blinded when a
policeman shot him in the face at close range said, "I feel what has brought my

eyesight back is to come here and tell the story. I feel what has been making me sick all the time is the fact that I couldn't tell my story. But now it feels like I've got my sight back by coming here and telling you the story."

Why is being heard so healing? I don't know the full answer to that question, but I do know it has something to do with the fact that listening creates relationship. We know from science that nothing in the universe exists as an isolated or independent entity. Everything takes form from relationships, be it subatomic particles sharing energy or ecosystems sharing food. In the web of life, nothing living lives alone.

Our natural state is to be together. In this time when we keep moving away from each other, we haven't lost the need and longing to be in relationship. Everybody has a story, and everybody wants to tell their story in order to connect. If no one listens, we tell it to ourselves and then we go mad. In the English language, the word for *health* comes from the same root as the word for *whole*. We can't be healthy if we're not in a relationship. And *whole* is from the same root word as *holy*.

Listening moves us closer; it helps us become more whole, more healthy, more holy. Not listening creates fragmentation, and fragmentation is the root of all suffering. Archbishop Desmond Tutu describes this era as a time of "radical brokenness" in all our relationships. Anywhere we look in the global family we see disconnection and fear of one another. For example, how many teenagers today, in many lands, state that no one listens to them? They feel ignored and discounted, and in pain they turn to each other to create their own subcultures, or they turn inside and commit suicide. I've heard two great teachers, Malidoma Somé from Burkino Fasso in West Africa and Parker Palmer from the United States, both make this comment: "You can tell a culture is in trouble when its elders walk across the street to avoid meeting its youth." It is impossible to create a healthy culture if we refuse to meet, and if we refuse to listen. But if we meet, and we listen, we reweave the world into wholeness. And holiness.

This is an increasingly noisy era—people shout at each other in print, at work, on TV. I believe the volume is directly related to our need to be listened to. In public places, in the media, we reward the loudest and most outrageous. People are literally clamoring for attention, and they'll do whatever it takes to be noticed. Things will only get louder until we figure out how to sit down and listen. Most of us would welcome things quieting down. We can do our part to begin lowering the volume by our own willingness to listen.

A schoolteacher told me how one day a sixteen-year-old became disruptive— shouting angrily, threatening her verbally. She could have called the authori- ties—there were laws to protect her from such abuse. Instead, she sat down and asked the student to talk to her. It took some time for him to quiet down, as he was very agitated and kept pacing the room. But finally he walked over to her and began talking about his life. She just listened. No one had listened to him in a long time. Her attentive silence gave him space to see himself, to hear himself. She didn't offer advice. She couldn't figure out his life, and she didn't have to. He could do it himself once she had listened.

I love the biblical passage "Whenever two or more are gathered, I am there." It describes for me the holiness of moments of real listening. The health, whole- ness, holiness of a new relationship forming. When we listen, we don't have to like the story or even the person telling their story. But listening creates a relationship. We move closer to one another.

In the field of restorative justice, victims of a crime meet with the ones who committed the crime. Parents whose child was murdered meet with the murderer. In this unimaginable setting, questions are asked and information exchanged. A young man who killed another teenager learns of who she was and what her loss means to her family, things he never thought about when he pulled the trigger. A rapist hears what it feels like to be raped, something he never knew, and also shares the blind rage that prompted his actions. Time after time, people who could be expected to fear and hate one another end up in relationships characterized by understanding and forgiveness.

I would like to encourage us all to play our part in the great healing that needs to occur everywhere. Think about whom you might approach—someone you don't know, don't like, or whose manner of living is a mystery to you. What would it take to begin a conversation with that person? Would you be able to ask him or her for an opinion or explanation, and then sit quietly to listen to the answer? Could you keep yourself from arguing, or defending, or saying anything for a while? Could you encourage the person to just keep telling you his or her version of things, that one side of the story?

It takes courage to begin this type of conversation. But listening, rather than arguing, also is much easier. Once I'd practiced this new role a few times, I found it quite enjoyable. And I learned things I never would have known had I interrupted or advised.

I know now that neither I nor the world changes from my well-reasoned, passionately presented arguments. Things change when I've created even just a slight movement toward wholeness, when I move closer to another through my patient, willing listening.

Raising Our Children

I keep noticing many disturbing indicators that things are not well in the lives of American children, including my own. By themselves, any of these incidents might mean little, but together they paint a disturbing picture. They indicate that children's lives have become miniature versions of our own lives.

Here are just a few incidents that I've noted:

— A New Jersey school system decides to give all children one free night with no scheduled activities. They have to plan for this six months in advance.

— Elementary school children are developing back and neck problems normally not seen until adulthood. These physical ailments are caused by their school backpacks. The packs often weigh about twenty pounds; the children often weigh about sixty pounds.

— Fourteen hundred college students died in 2002 as a consequence of binge drinking. Out-of-control college drinking on campuses has become so serious that congressional hearings have been held to investigate its causes.

— My thirteen-year-old granddaughter explained to me how she needs to know her weekly schedule; otherwise she can't cope with the anxiety and develops headaches.

Obviously, children no longer have to wait until adulthood to feel overcommitted and overwhelmed. Even before they start school, children develop schedules of their own, moving from one coordinated activity or program to another. We seem to be acculturating our children to be constantly busy, to be burdened by schedules, to become so stressed that they seek inappropriate and harmful ways to release that stress.

I don't know if there's a solution to this frenzy of activity at all ages. But even if we can't save ourselves, please let's notice what's happening to our children. How do our children deal with unstructured time? Do they ever have quiet moments, when nothing's going on? How do they feel when their plans fall apart? What's their response to boredom and loneliness?

Lest I sound like a crabby old lady, let me tell you why I started noticing these things. I spend a great deal of time with teenagers, partly because I have two, and partly because they were both in a rock band, and I often traveled to concerts and clubs where they performed. I also have fourteen grandchildren. And my work brings me into daily contact with many adults in different professions and workplaces. During the past few years, I've watched the levels of stress, anxiety, conflict, and craziness keep rising in these different age groups.

There are many indicators of escalating stress. In America and Europe, sleeping disorders are on the rise, rage and abuse are on the rise. More diseases are appearing that are linked to nervous conditions. One European health survey predicted that within the next twenty years, the leading causes of death would be from diseases of the heart and of the nervous system. Teachers report greater anxiety in students. Some of this is a manifestation of their parents' stress; some of it is caused by the demands placed on kids. Increasingly, greater numbers of children are medicated in order to quiet them down and to help them stay focused.

From what I observe, American society is speeding up to such a frenzy that, any day now, I expect to witness a human being exploding in front of me. And when this frenzy starts to affect our children, when we unconsciously create them in our own image, I get worried. It's been a slow creeping change in our children's lives, the boiled frog who didn't notice the water temperature rising. When did it become normal for kids to have so many commitments in their lives that they require their own schedules and day planners? When did we develop the expectation that kids should do so many activities: school work, organized league sports, school clubs, music, dance or sports lessons, paying jobs, and active social lives? It's no wonder that many high school students report they stay up doing homework well past midnight. Homework is the last obligation at the end of a day of nonstop activities. And parents of young children are encouraged to get them involved in structured programs and lessons even before they begin school. (Let me confess: I had one son in swimming lessons at six months. One daughter-in-law teaches music and rhythm to children one to three years of age.)

Most parents I know are not happy with the pace of their kids' demanding schedules. Early evenings and weekends are spent shuttling kids to their sporting events or school activities. It's no wonder we can't wait for them to be able to drive. But even if we want to slow things down and give our kids some relief, most of them don't want it.

As hassled and fatigued as our kids may be, they've grown dependent on feeling busy. They've learned to schedule their days down to the minute in order to fit in everything. They don't know what to do with down time. Several of the students interviewed in New Jersey found that the free evening given to them by their community was boring. They felt confined by "free" time.

So changing our kids' lives is very complex. They don't know what they're missing. And peer pressure is real. Therefore, we can't act individually as parents and insist that only our kids participate in fewer activities. If we ask them to withdraw from "normal" activities, they'll only feel strange, different, and alienated from us. The community in New Jersey realized that this was a community issue and made an attempt to address it at that level.

Because this is a community issue, we need to start the conversation with other parents and with school administrators. If we share our own experiences, we can better notice what's going on. Then together we can determine what we might initiate as a community to ease up on our kids.

I hope we don't have to wait until our children reach adulthood for them to discover that a healthy life requires peaceful moments, and that being present in the moment is a wondrous skill. I hope we can teach them that plans are not the answer to all of life's needs, that there is truth to the old joke that if you want to make God laugh, just present your plans. I hope we can teach them to expect moments of chaos when everything falls apart and to dance with those moments rather than fear them. I hope we can teach them to not be afraid of boredom and loneliness, so that they stop grasping after entertainment, drugs, or alcohol to fill the void. Loneliness, boredom, restlessness—these are conditions of being human. No matter how much we deny them or run from them, they always return. As we mature, hopefully we learn that we don't need to fill the emptiness, that we can just sit with it and it will pass.

But I wonder how my children are learning these fundamental life lessons.

Ending Our Silence

Eight hundred years ago, Catherine of Sienna, who was later canonized as a Catholic saint, stated, "Speak the truth in a million voices. It is silence that kills." Her words haunt me today, as I notice how much silence there is and how it is growing around the world. This silence, like a thickening fog, is becoming visible in many places.

— At an international peace conference in Croatia, participants were asked, "What keeps you from speaking up for peace?"

— At an educator's conference in the United States, a well-known champion of public education confronted his audience with three important issues that no one was talking about, behavior he dubbed as "our great silences."

— In Europe, many people express remorse that their nations stayed silent as war in the Balkans escalated. Why didn't they act to prevent the atrocities and massacres of the Bosnian war? (The United Nations issued a formal apology for its failure to prevent the massacre in Srebrenica.)

— In Africa, both Europe and the United States keep expressing regret for not intervening to stop the slaughter of millions in Rwanda, or the Sudan, or Sierra Leone. But the slaughter continues.

— In a rural Kenyan village, a young African woman dying of AIDS wonders why America is so silent on the AIDS pandemic. She asks her sister who lives in Seattle, "Does anybody know that we're dying?"

Why is silence moving like a fog across the planet? Why is it growing in us as individuals, even as we learn of more and more issues that concern us? Why do we fail to raise our voice on behalf of things that trouble us, and then regret what we didn't do? As I've watched the silence grow in myself and others, I've noticed a few reasons for the silence, but none of these are entirely sufficient as explanations.

We don't know how to talk to each other anymore. Even in nations where there is a strong tradition of citizen participation, people have stopped talking to one another about the most troubling political issues. A Danish woman explained that political correctness made people fearful to engage in conversations about the influx of immigrants that is impacting Denmark's homogenous culture, forcing them to deal with diversity and inclusion. She explained that since reasonable people failed to talk about this issue, right wing splinter groups have developed, marketing fear-based, exclusionary solutions. As she described this behavior, it felt like an accurate description of what's happened in many democratic societies. The silence of thoughtful people creates a vacuum filled by extremists.

We're overwhelmed by the amount of suffering in the world. It's impossible to notice what's going on in the world during this dark age without feeling overwhelmed and helpless. There are very few true solutions. Most solutions only result in more complex problems, and every act of compassion is countered by more acts of aggression and greed. The sheer number of problems, and their unending nature and global scale, has pushed many of us into silence. It is too much to bear, and so we choose numbness over involvement.

People feel more powerless now than at any time in recent history. Recently I was in a conversation with twenty-five people, ages twenty-two to sixty, from fifteen different countries. I was saddened to hear that all but one of us shared the same experience—we do not feel represented by our governments, and we feel powerless to change this. Decisions are being made in our name that we absolutely disagree with. As one young leader from England now living in

Holland remarked: "I see all these decisions being made by men in ties. I feel so angry. I see the youth not being heard, getting pissed off and going to the streets in protest, and look at what happens to them!"

We're afraid of what we might lose if we speak out. A young Ecuadorian environmentalist working for her government described how she couldn't get support from local environmental organizations because they were afraid they might lose their government funds. The U.S. educator who named "our great silences" noted that educators fear the loss of funding or favors if they question current policies. In the sixties, this was called "being co-opted," forfeiting one's integrity and principles in order to stay on the good side of those in power. Since then, co-optation seems to have become far more prevalent, just more subtle. We hesitate to challenge those who offer us employment, funds, or respectability. We want to see change, justice, peace, but delude ourselves into thinking these can occur with no cost to ourselves.

We've convinced ourselves that what is happening elsewhere doesn't affect us. Perhaps we're still denying our interconnectedness, believing that things happening far away do not threaten us. Or perhaps we're grasping for whatever personal benefits we can while we still have time, sensing that things are only getting worse.

I had a personal wake-up call about silence and giving voice several years ago, when I was working with a colleague from South Africa. It was just eighteen months after the elections that brought Nelson Mandela and black South Africans to power. My friend, like many white South Africans, was just then learning the details of apartheid, the system under which he, as a white, had prospered, while millions had suffered so horribly. As more and more atrocities were revealed, his twenty-seven-year-old son confronted him one day: "How could you not have known what was going on? How could you not know?" I was sitting in the serene comfort of a conference room in America when I heard this story. But the question pierced right through me. I knew in that moment that I never wanted to be in the position of my friend, that I never wanted to be confronted by my own children or grandchildren.

Since then, I do not always speak up for all the issues and problems that disturb me. I give voice to some and not for others. I can't pretend that I make rational choices, where I "choose my battles." Sometimes I am just too tired to care; sometimes I lack courage; sometimes I notice that others have picked up that cause and I don't have to. But at least I now notice when I remain silent and am more conscious that silence is a choice I make. I'm learning that silence is not the absence of action, but another form of action. And I hold myself accountable for that.

The eighteenth-century historian Edmund Burke said it clearly: "The only thing necessary for the triumph of evil is for good men to do nothing." I hope that I am doing what I can, although it may not be enough. And if my grandchildren one day come to me and ask, "Why didn't you do something?" at least I will be able to tell them what I did.

Everything Has a Deep Dream

by Rachel Naomi Remen

I've spent many years learning
how to fix life, only to discover
at the end of the day
that life is not broken.

There is a hidden seed of greater wholeness
in everyone and everything.
We serve life best
when we water it
and befriend it.
When we listen before we act.

In befriending life,
we do not make things happen
according to our own design.
We uncover something that is already happening
    in us and around us and
create conditions that enable it.

Everything is moving toward its place of wholeness
always struggling against odds.

Everything has a deep dream of itself and its fulfillment.

Note: Prose passage in *My Grandfather's Blessing* (p. 247) redone as a poem by Meg Wheatley.

My Own Footsteps

These are personal essays, things I see that I feel compelled to comment on. They focus on my hope and my distress, on my children, on my nation, on those I've met in other countries, and on those I've learned from who come from many different traditions. They chronicle a few of my most poignant moments—some joyful, some agonizing, each one filled with paradox. I continue to swim willingly in the spiral of paradox. I've learned that it is these explorations that yield the great blessings of peace and renewed dedication to finding our way.

We were together. I forget the rest.

—attributed to Walt Whitman

Consumed by Either Fire or Fire: Journeying with T. S. Eliot

For too long, I have lived in the world wanting to change it. This has been an impossible stance. It takes normal desires to contribute something to the human condition and intensifies them into crusades that are doomed to disappoint. I have gradually weaned myself from this posture, I think, because it is just too exhausting and unsatisfying.

As I've traveled this road that I made hard, I've had many essential friends. Including T. S. Eliot. I cannot avoid him. Time and again I get absorbed in the relentless weaving of paradox and imagery in *Four Quartets*. Many times I have used Eliot to provoke my own experience—to understand what I've learned about this work of wanting the world to be different, better. Eliot shines brilliant beams of light on the path I've been exploring. He names sensations I experience as I discover how best to direct my energy and passion. Sensations that began as pain or wonder, that now sometimes sleep quietly within as wisdom gained, questions answered.

As I was reading him yet again, I began copying those passages that always leap out at me. Certain lines endure as a meaningful chronicle of my experience, expressed in his voice far beyond my own capacity for expression. I became engaged in a dialogue with myself (undoubtedly the easiest kind to have) about why these lines keep attracting me.

I know that we notice what we notice because of who we are. We create ourselves by what we *choose* to notice. Once this work of self-authorship has begun, we inhabit the world we've created. We self-seal. We don't notice anything except those things that confirm what we already think about who we already are. But I've always appreciated the thought of the semanticist I. A. Richards, who describes a good reader as "a mind paying attention to itself." Using more in terms of his field of semantics, he speaks of what meditative traditions call the observer self. When we succeed in moving outside our normal processes of self-reference and can look at ourselves with self-awareness, then we have a chance at changing. We break the seal. We notice something new.

So I'm wondering now what newness I will notice as I go back into *Four Quartets*. If I contemplate those descriptions of his world that I chose to notice, will I then see mine differently? I want to follow Eliot's lead on this journey. I want to enter the endless spiral of his paradoxes to see what I will see. And from this, I hope to enlarge the paradoxes I embrace as I draw the circle of self.

> You say I am repeating
> Something I have said before. I shall say it again.
> Shall I say it again? In order to arrive there,
> To arrive where you are, to get from where you are
> not,
> You must go by a way wherein there is no ecstasy.
> In order to arrive at what you do not know
> You must go by a way which is the way of ignorance.
> In order to possess what you do not possess
> You must go by the way of dispossession.
> In order to arrive at what you are not
> You must go through the way in which you are not.
> And what you do not know is the only thing you know
> And what you own is what you do not own
> And where you are is where you are not.
> —"East Coker III"

I choose to begin with this passage not because of its profound paradox, but because it begins with irony and frustration. I appreciate these emotions as frequent companions of paradox. I relate to his repetition, because I find myself in many different places, repeating myself. And I'm frustrated with repeating myself (I shall say it again. Shall I say it again?) because I know I'm saying things that have been said by others, over and over. I'm giving voice to ideas that have been expressed by mystics, martyrs, philosophers, scientists, and everyday people. For millennia. Is anybody listening?

I lose my patience. I wonder where all the learning is going, why it isn't showing up in new beliefs, new practices. Patience is my greatest challenge. (Well, actually, the challenge is compassion, from which patience arises.) So I try to relearn patience from the true exemplars, those spiritual teachers past and present who spend their whole ministries being repetitious. They never accuse us of being stupid or stubborn. These teachers so love the truth of what they say that they seem to enjoy repeating themselves. I think this must be the key. Loving truth so much that no repetition is tedious. Feeling truth new and vibrant each time it is voiced. Loving people so well that giving voice energizes the speaker long past normal human endurance.

Well, maybe.

What are the truths that Eliot must keep repeating? He follows with a timeless description of the path by which truth is obtained. Pure paradox, a path that jostles us continually with its demands. A path that requires no less than the total loss of certainty and identity. "A condition of complete simplicity (Costing not less than everything)," he says at the very end of the Quartets. The way of no ecstasy, the way of ignorance and not-knowing, the path of dispossession and the dissolution of self that opens us to life.

Many years ago when I was first beginning writing about new science, the journey ahead was described to me in one trenchant phrase: This was a journey "of wonder and not-knowing." I have remained clear about that, and perhaps in contradiction to Eliot, I have found that wonderment, which opens us to new truth, is often accompanied by something a bit like ecstasy. Astonishment is fun; people love the experience. Wonder seems to return us to our innocence. We enter into a state of delight—show us something else strange and preposterous so that we can laugh and exclaim. In this innocent state, we are willing to give up our self-concepts and glimpse into the unknown with new eyes. Ever since I began noticing the effects of wonder, I've tried to lead people to a place where they could encounter this astonishing world and grin with delight. If I could do that, I learned they would willingly follow me elsewhere in thought.

But the rest of the journey is just as Eliot describes it. He is, after all, repeating the paradoxes of Jesus, of Buddha, of Lao Tzu. If you would save your life, you must lose it. If you would thrive in the new world, you must dissolve your old form. Letting go is the only path to safety. Surrounded by so much truth, it's a puzzle how we ever came to deny it. Did we ever really believe we could proceed through life by growing all the time, new and improved at every turn? How did the shadow disappear from our pursuit of the light? When did we forget that "there must be opposition in all things"? When did we stop acknowledging the great space for discovery that is created by the opposing poles of paradox?

> I said to my soul, be still, and wait without hope
> for hope would be hope for the wrong thing; wait without
> love
> For love would be love of the wrong thing; there is yet faith
> But the faith and the love and the hope are all in the waiting.
> Wait without thought, for you are not ready for thought:
> So the darkness shall be the light, and the stillness the dancing.
> —"East Coker III"

Eliot extends his hand and asks us to dance into the emptying stillness that truth places on our path. We cannot approach truth from who we are. We think too small. We are confined and confining in our beliefs. A few years ago, feeling imprisoned by the beliefs I was promulgating passionately to myself and to the world, I imagined creating a year-end ritual. I've never done it in all the glorious pomp and pageant I imagined, but the ritual is "The Bonfire of Beliefs." At least once a year, can I take those ideas and beliefs I most cherish and try to see the world without them? "For hope would be hope for the wrong thing . . . for love would be love of the wrong thing." Give up what I believe—these truths are too small for me to perceive what I truly seek. Open to something much wilder, although that too will become tame. Do this over and over, until I ring inside from hollowness and emptied faith. Except the faith I learn in the waiting. Real faith.

> We must be still and still moving
> Into another intensity
> For a further union, a deeper communion
> Through the dark cold and the empty desolation,
> The wave cry, the wind cry, the vast waters
> Of the petrel and the porpoise. In my end is my beginning.
> —"East Coker V"

The journey is the accumulation of stillness. Patience. Emptiness. The union that I seek is not of my creation. The self I have created impedes union. Stillness must be learned, and the endless time in which I learn it is filled with doubts and desolations. Stillness often feels like abandonment. Why isn't Spirit communicating with me? What have I done to deserve such a stony, cold silence? How do I avoid filling with new terrors the emptiness that terrifies me?

Yet the wave cry and the wind cry want to fill the silence. Life is our comforter. When I stop the self-absorption, when I can pause a moment to gaze on what's around me, I experience this comfort. I feel the movement of forces that exist beyond me, but which willingly carry me with them. I don't experience nature's elemental energies of wind, movement, or mountains cast high into the sky as hostile. In that, I may be lucky—never to have been over-whelmed by gales or floods. When I lift my head into the wind, or commune with a mountain, I do so as a participant. I feel this planet as an expression of the life that moves in me and everyone. Often, Nature is my most comforting companion. She invites me to remember that I am necessary to creation.

But only if I discipline myself to stop looking inward. Only if I remember that the communion I seek is everywhere around me, waiting for me to notice its presence. It is another intensity and it cries out for us.

> And what you thought you came for
> Is only a shell, a husk of meaning
> From which the purpose breaks only when it is fulfilled
> If at all. Either you had no purpose
> Or the purpose is beyond the end you figured
> And is altered in fulfillment.
> —"Little Gidding I"

Here is life's great gift—unending surprise. And its other gift—inherent orderli-ness. We are not adrift in a purposeless universe. We are not the by-product of a Darwinian accident that felt lucky because we were the ones to survive. I used to challenge MBA students with the question "Do you think your life's purpose is something you create or discover?" They always wheedled out of it by answering, "Both." This may be true, but I feel that Viktor Frankl was right when he said that "meaning precedes being." I know we each have a unique contribution that is necessary for the whole of us to thrive. I know our gifts are required. I don't know where these gifts originate, but I know what they feel like. I feel joyful when I yield to their expression.

Yet Eliot cautions us about something I also know to be true. We so want to know our purpose that we too quickly determine what we think it is, and we kill ourselves in the process. We turn from stillness and listening to earnest action, and Spirit disappears. After a while we find ourselves expired—we played God with our lives and lost the source of all inspiration, the breath of life.

This is a real dilemma. How do we attend to our purpose while holding the humility that we do not create it? Once we catch a glimmer of what it might be, how do we avoid taking over as creator? It gets even more complicated. How do we avoid getting ego seduced by the specific manifestation of our gifts? Is it possible to live in the humility of knowing that our purpose, as clearly as we self-define it, is but "a husk of meaning"? The task is really to become superb listeners. The German philosopher Heidegger wrote that waiting, listening, was the most profound way to serve God.

Can we live into the presence of purpose, never hoping for a straightforward answer but inviting always the great mystery that gives rise to our questions?

> You are not here to verify,
> Instruct yourself, or inform curiosity
> Or carry report. You are here to kneel
> Where prayer has been valid.
> —"Little Gidding I"

To this place, listening carries us. Whatever we conceive our work to be, in the end we know that we are only, infinitely, serving the place of prayer. I used to believe my work was about organizations and life inside them. Then a bit later I thought I was charged with changing the dominant worldview of Western thought. Notice how my scope increased as my ego gained a surer footing. Then one day, in a sunny patch of jungle in the Yucatan, I leaned against a small but perfect Mayan ruin while my two sons swam in a shadowy cave pool. Faced with jungle growth and sun, and the cold stones of yet another attempt at civilization, I knew that my work was, as is everyone's, about reclaiming Life. All of us are struggling together toward a time when the human spirit can find more room for itself in the societies we create. We are all participating in enlarging the spaces in which we together dwell, so that they might hold more of the greatness of each of us.

> Who then devised the torment? Love.
> Love is the unfamiliar Name
> Behind the hands that wove
> The intolerable shirt of flame
> Which human power cannot remove.
> We only live, only suspire
> Consumed by either fire or fire.
> —"Little Gidding IV"

I lose my breath reading this passage. Do I experience the demands of Love as an intolerable shirt of flame? I know I feel there is no escape from this path, but I don't yet know that this path leads only to fire. I do, more and more, feel as my companions those from all centuries who followed the blinding path of Love, who willingly donned the shirt of flame and wore it to their martyrdom. Recently I've been reflecting on how strange we are, my generation, to believe we can help birth a new world without it affecting our career progress. I'm aware of how little courage our lives have required of us. But Life keeps raising the stakes.

When I thought the opposition to my work was in the person of a controlling boss, it seemed I might maneuver my way past him or her. When I thought the opposition originated from a lack of evidence for how much we all benefit from inclusive, inviting workplaces, it seemed I might create change by rational argument. When I thought the work was about shifting a worldview and welcoming in life's great creative capacities to our human lives, it seemed I had a lot of support from the planetary community of living beings. They were making their case—I needed merely to direct attention to what they were doing.

But Love is not satisfied by logic. It may be that we'll accomplish this latest revolution with grace, that we'll marshal the powers of nonviolence and people will willingly surrender their ideas and their power because they too are tired of the violence and the impotence. But maybe not. Maybe the only route to Love is fire, or fire. I don't know this, but I do know that I have had to surrender to this as the great possibility. I have had to confront whether I am willing, if asked, to forego the life that holds me so securely and comfortably. And I don't know what I have answered, because Life hasn't yet asked me. I believe I have recognized the shirt of flame, but will I be asked to wear it?

But Eliot has moved beyond my question, put my queries to rest. He has illuminated the path and assured me of the journey. I have learned what we are engaged in and how we must be together.

> There is only the fight to recover what has been lost
> And found and lost again and again: and now, under
> conditions
> That seem unpropitious. But perhaps neither gain nor loss.
> For us, there is only the trying. The rest is not our business.
> —"East Coker V"

This is the knowing that resolves paradox, that puts an end to questions. Shall I say it again? I shall say it again. We do what we are called to do because we feel called to do it. We walk silently, willingly, down the well-trodden path still lit by the fire of millions. And the rest, I know now, is not our business.

Maybe You Will Be the Ones:
To My Sons and Their Friends

I am on Lake Powell in the southwestern United States, drifting along the border of Utah and Arizona, wondering about America's next fifty years. I am floating in deep red rock canyons that are several hundred million years old. Whenever I look up from my computer, I see awesome slick rock wantonly displaying its entire evolutionary history.

These rocks are here today because the beaches of ancient seas were compressed into sedimentary rock that formed into thousands of layers that then were uplifted by massive earth upheavals to form these towering red mountains, which were carved into canyons by relentless rivers ten million years ago.

I tell this just to keep things in perspective.

Lake Powell highlights more than evolutionary time—it was created by human imagination wedded to unwavering arrogance. In the 1950s, American engineers dammed several canyons and rivers in order to produce electricity, create reservoirs and develop recreational areas. Lake Powell was created by flooding Glen Canyon. Next on the list to be dammed was the Grand Canyon! We were spared that incomprehensible act because of public outrage at the loss of Glen Canyon.

This lake is a dramatic testament to the troubling American impulse to use our technology and daring to coerce nature to our own purposes, our belief that the planet is here for whatever use we can make of it. And while the red rocks witness the planet's creative forces, they also alert us to the historic moment we occupy now. For the first time, the consequences of our acts affect the entire planet, all peoples and all beings.

As I imagine what the next fifty years might bring, I know that either we will have learned to be responsible planetary stewards of our human creativity, or we will have wreaked unimaginable havoc with our only home. But however we humans behave, the rocks will continue their cycles of emergence and disintegration.

America's Uniqueness

Human creativity thrives in the United States. We entice millions to our shores by its magical lure. As a nation, we have given the world many things, and paramount is our focus on individual freedom that has allowed imagination to soar and explore the limitless sky of human creativity.

Nowhere else have I experienced the boundless sense of possibility that is so easily available in Americans. We are the most optimistic nation on earth, and people risk everything to get here so that they might breathe in this great space of possibility.

American creativity has given birth to this interconnected world that is changing the pace, the rules, and the meaning of modern life. It is a world filled with paradox. We can reach out to the planet to play chess on the Web with people in Turkey, but we have less time to play games with our own kids. Those with a good idea hope to become rich, yet we have less time to think and develop knowledge and wisdom. We realize that we live in a web of life, that our actions have impact around the globe, yet we continue to act in competitive and nonsystemic ways and to greedily use most of the world's resources.

In the next several years, America will need to resolve these paradoxes. Can we use the gift of our freedom and imagination not just to create a new economy, but to create a world that works for all?

Conversations with Teens

Lake Powell is not my only companion as I think about this question. I am spending the week on a fifty-four-foot houseboat with thirteen teenage boys between the ages of fifteen and twenty (two are my sons). Lest you doubt my sanity, know that I learned a long time ago that my teenage sons move as a clan, comfortable and happy only when surrounded by friends. This vacation was planned for the clan, not our family, and I am having a wonderful time on this houseboat experiencing life as lived by strong, creative, young American men.

How things evolve, and whether we will successfully resolve our current paradoxes, depends on the young men and women who are now in our junior and senior high schools. Realizing that I am surrounded on this houseboat by those who will help birth the future, I put aside my notes and ask if we can talk. Some are already gathered in the cabin, and I ask them to tell me what they imagine for the future. What do they want the world to be like when they are sixty-five?

Within minutes of beginning this conversation, the other boys flock in, and soon all thirteen teenagers are gathered around. For the next hour I just listen to them, honored that they want to be in this conversation with me. I revel in how intent they are, how no one drifts out of the room, how much they love being asked their views on something this big and important, how most of them have very strong views about the future, how they're in this conversation with each other, not just me. This is what I hear them say:

They want less hate. They fear for the planet. They want robots to do dull work. They want schools to stop being so awful. They expect pure (electronic) democracy by then. They want to stop violence. They want to stop being desensitized by the media to violence, suffering, warfare. They want families. They want to be loving, supportive parents. They want to stop taking America for granted.

I ask them what do you hope for? They reply:

I want to know I've given my best, no matter what. I want a lot less negativity. I want the second coming of Christ. I want to know that I have encouraged another human being. I want children. I'm afraid to have children. I want something to happen that will unite us as humans—maybe this will happen if we make contact with extraterrestrials. I want to end the greed of corporations. I want to teach my family good values. I believe one person can make a difference, like Gandhi did. I don't think one person can do anything. I want us to stop being hypocrites and to take responsibility for our own behavior.

Paradoxical Lives

Who are these children, these thirteen boys camped on a houseboat among ancient rocks looking into their future? They are wonderfully American— among these thirteen is one South African immigrant, one first-generation American with parents from Argentina and the Cherokee and Chickasaw nations, many of northern and southern European descent, one with Choctaw nation ancestors, and one descendant of Ulysses S. Grant.

President Grant's descendant has had a difficult life and is in foster care. Many of the others (including my two sons) are children of divorce. Socioeconomic status ranges from struggling to make ends meet to easy affluence. About a third are finishing high school through nontraditional programs, home study, or GED.

And they are representative of America in other ways. We all agree that we are living the American paradox. We know the things we do are destructive to the planet or use too many of the world's resources, yet we can't stop loving the life we live. We want to help the environment, but every day of this vacation, we're burning up thirty gallons of carbon-based fuels to play on jet skis.

We want a world that works for all, but we willingly consume far too much of the world's resources as evident in our daily three bags of garbage. We know the earth is running out of critical resources such as water, but we ourselves run out of water on the boat because we don't monitor our usage.

We want everyone in this world to enjoy a better life, but we can't stop ourselves from living a life that we know is destructive to others.

One other thing I notice about them, not only in this conversation, is the quality of their relationships. Instead of the anticipated contesting, competing, and generally macho behavior, I observe consistent levels of support and concern. When one young man freezes on a cliff, paralyzed by vertigo, three others talk with him patiently and lovingly to help him down. Vertigo strikes him a second time on another hike, and again I witness an intense effort to help him. These incidents are never thrown in his face.

And they don't even notice how different they are from earlier generations when competition kept people separate from each other. At night, they sit on the roof of the boat and write music together. There's no sense of individual ownership. One person develops a musical theme, others chime in with their instruments, and they banter back and forth—playful, excited, complementing each other.

They love to create together. I watch them composing together, coaching each other, teaching each other, admiring each other's talents. I admire their talents. One is a genius at creating Web sites. Several are musicians, two are writers, one never leaves his computer games, and many play high school football. All in all, they are funny, talented and astonishingly convivial—with me, each other, and any adult who will pause to talk with them.

A Boundaryless World
These young people care about each other. I am surprised by their skills at human psychology. They seem to know what's going on at deeper levels, using

this awareness to explain each other's motivation—why someone is doing what he's doing. When any two start arguing or become angry at each other, others step forward to help them work it out. I'm amazed at how well they process things, listening to all sides, figuring out ways to move into new behaviors, creating compromises. They are far more skilled than many adults I know.

Most of these children are embodiments of American optimism. They believe in themselves, each other, and the future. But they do not seem to act from the same fierce nationalism that has plagued many earlier generations, including mine. Their hearts are more wide open.

The world they know is much smaller than the one I grew up in. They are connected to children all over the world through a global teen culture of music, movies, and sports. Many of us have (quite rightly) decried the loss of local cultures and the Americanization of the planet, but when I observe how easily my sons talk with teens they meet in Brazil or Zimbabwe or Europe, I realize something good is happening as well. They don't have the concept of "foreigner." Their world isn't filled with strangers. They can talk instantly about a musician or a movie and have an energetic conversation that dissolves cultural differences.

As these children create the new world, I know they will help create a networked, boundaryless world. My generation has tossed these words around, but these kids live it. Even when they develop into tight groups, cliques, and gangs, they know there's a big world out there that is as close as their music, TV, phones, or computer screen.

So are my boat companions a "normal" group of teenagers? I hope so. I think these kids are quite typical, and I feel extraordinarily privileged to have lived with them so intimately for six days.

My Response

Here is what I want to say to them directly.

Thank you for letting me see you. Thank you for being people who are fun to be with, think with, and dream with. Thank you above all for not taking at face value what my generation has believed and tried so hard to teach you. We would have you believe that the world is ruled by competition, that only the strong survive, that you must look out always and only for yourself, that to succeed in this world you must practice deceit, greed, selfishness, and violence.

We haven't taught you well about honor, sustainability, community, or compassion. We failed to show you how to be wise stewards of the earth, how to care for one another, how to resolve conflicts peacefully, how to enjoy others' creativity as well as your own.

Yet miraculously, you are learning these things. These more humane capacities have captured your attention, more than our incessant messages to the contrary. Maybe you're reacting to watching your parents' compulsive pursuit of self-interest and individualism. Maybe you're expressing the fundamental need of humans to be together. (For eons, we humans have struggled to live together even as we've fought to be apart.)

I am excited that you seem to be figuring it out for yourself. I only want to encourage you in the direction you're already moving. If you pay attention to certain strengths you already have, then I believe that the future we talked about is truly possible.

Three Critical Strengths

Here is one strength I see. You know how to enjoy each other's gifts. You don't feel diminished by each other's talents. You take delight if one of you is a great guitarist, one writes terrific songs, one doesn't like music but loves computers, one plays sports, one plays computer games. You don't need to be alike. You seem to know that your diverse talents are your collective strength. I love how you revel in your diversity—something that other generations haven't figured out.

If you keep enjoying how individual uniqueness adds to your collective ability, you will have moved past one of the most troubling issues of this time, this new millennium when there are wars in nearly one-fourth of all countries. Maybe you will be the ones to help all humans take the leap into the great gift of human diversity.

Another strength: You know that you need each other. I believe we adults have inadvertently helped you here. We have ignored you, denied you, seen you as a problem. You learned to stay together because older generations couldn't or wouldn't invite you to join them. (Outside Columbine High School, you huddled in each other's arms, consoling each other into sudden adulthood in a world where violence was random but *did* make sense.)

I believe you understand more about the terrors of separation than I do. You experience so much violence, so much stereotyping, so much exclusion, that many of you know firsthand that feeling separate does terrible things to the human spirit. I hope you can carry that awareness with you into adulthood. I hope you are the ones who hold onto each other and refuse to move into the competitive space of feeling better than, feeling different from, feeling holier than.

To succeed where all others have failed, you will have to hold onto your present sense of outrage over exclusion and turn that anger into compassion. You will have to keep your hearts open rather than contract them. You will have to help rather than judge the kids around you who choose to protect themselves by forming exclusionary groups.

And I hope you remember, as you said on the boat, that "you can't solve violence with more violence."

Another strength: You love creating and you claim that freedom. You do not tolerate nearly as much confinement, rules, repressive structures as your parents and I did. You walk away from disrespectful employers, boring work, uninteresting activities. As parents, we have been quick to criticize you. We fear you have no work ethic, no standards, no values. But you make me hopeful because your refusal to conform and comply might save you from being diminished.

I see you standing up for who you are, I see you reclaiming the freedom and respect that every human spirit requires if it is to flourish. If you are successful here, you will have claimed a future where many more people feel welcome to offer their unique creative gifts.

The Next Leap
Here is something I'm not sure you know. These three strengths only work together. Things go terribly wrong when just one is emphasized. Many generations and civilizations have failed because they supported only one of these essential aspects of human nature.

For example, in the United States, we have fought to develop and sustain individual freedom and we've ended up with a litigious society where everyone knows their rights, but few know how to be in a community. Yet many indigenous cultures believe that individual gifts belong to the community. Individuals lose personal freedom as they serve the community, not themselves. In other societies, people have strong relationships within their community, but create this collective by drawing hard barriers between themselves and others.

This is the world you grew up in, a world populated by enemies and strangers, where ethnic wars, genocides and border conflicts predominate.

And now it's your turn to experiment with the mystery of human society. What will be its next form? Maybe you will be the ones who learn how to weave these three strengths together, a creative spiral of our unique gifts, our desire for community, and our need for individual freedom. If you figure this out, we will move forward as a planetary community where people can experience what it means to be fully human.

I believe this is the next evolutionary leap of our species—how to take our diversity, our personal freedom, and our creativity and use it to create a plane-tary community where all life can flourish. No generation before you has figured this out, but we've chronicled our experiences and our history is there to help you.

None of these three human strengths is particular to Americans—they are common human longings—but because you are maturing in America, you have the gift of freedom and the opportunity to explore them, to observe them, to learn from others. In that way you are unique, and if you succeed, you will be creating a new world for all, not just for Americans. And I know you already know that.

In fifty years, maybe you'll be back on Lake Powell, again playing in the red rocks. If the lake is still here functioning as a healthy ecosystem, that will be the first sign that you have succeeded. And if you are still friends who want to be together, that will be the sign that you have truly succeeded.

Maybe you will be the ones. I pray that you are.

Postscript

Whenever possible in my work, I bring adults and teenagers together. This is easiest when working in communities or schools, but it's important to do everywhere. It always yields great value—much improved relationships and important new insights. Before they work together, adults and teens have fairly negative views about each other. And both groups lack skill in knowing how to talk with each other. Adults tend to pontificate; teens tend to tune out. But when engaged in a good process where they can listen to one another, it's a wondrous experience. The adults are amazed at what intelligent contributions the teens make; the teens are amazed to feel respected and listened to.

This essay represents the best about teenagers. Many adults don't know whether to share my optimism. And I didn't know if I'd been too optimistic. So I asked several teens whom I didn't know to read this essay, to see whether it felt true to them. I was surprised by their eagerness to comment. I've included some of their responses here, not to praise me but to reveal how teens see themselves, how they experience adults, and how much they want to contribute to society.

— "Teenagers are usually disregarded as great problems in our society because we supposedly have no work ethic, no standards, no values. This author actually has faith in teens and our ability to make a difference in our society."

— "Wheatley gives a positive view of teenagers today. She gives us the credit we deserve. This kind of acknowledgment encourages us to get out there and help the world become a better place."

— "It was uplifting to hear that Wheatley has faith in my generation. I can tell she cares not only about the future of the world but how we as young people can create it. I have been told countless times that my generation is the first to stand for nothing, that we are the consumer age lacking in morality and ambition. I strongly believe, and am inspired to do so by this [essay], that this idea is false. I look forward to proving everyone wrong. I think we are the ones to do it."

– "This [essay] is everything America needs to hear. I find this essay makes me excited to be seventeen and inspired to make our future better."

America's Dark Night

My nation now knows more about waging war than it does about anything else. We know what can be done with different guns, missiles, fighter planes, even the nicknames given to aircraft carriers. Retired military officers, now TV stars, have explained the details of battle strategy, demonstrated every weapon in America's arsenal, and paraded soldiers on morning TV wearing the newest battle gear.

I remember listening to a pilot on TV excitedly describe his night vision goggles, how he could see where his bombs landed. When the bombs hit, our TV screens showed only plumes of fire and shattered buildings floating eerily in the air. But this pilot saw the destruction in detail.

I remember using those same night vision goggles. It was 1993, and I was working for the U.S. Army's chief of staff. He had asked me to act as his scout, to look at several change initiatives in the army and tell him what I saw. So here I was, riding in a Hummer through the army's remote desert center for tank training. It was dark night. We rode in total blackout, not a light anywhere, night vision goggles on. At one point, I aimlessly raised my head and looked up. Instantly, the stars we can't see were glowing in my eyes. (Astronomers estimate that there are at least fifty million stars behind each one we can see.) I have never forgotten that rapturous glimpse into the universe provided by military technology. Or the paradox.

I experience this as a dark time for America, where we seem to have lost our way. I search to find the means for us to see clearly through the darkness. I want us to be able to see both the destruction, and the stars. I felt this even before we chose war, for more fundamental reasons. In the past several years,

America has embraced values that cannot create a sustainable society and world. We organize too many of our activities around beliefs that are inherently life destroying. We believe that growth can be endless, that competition creates healthy relationships, that consumption need have no limits, that meaning is found in things, that aggression brings peace. Societies that use these values end up, as do all predators in nature, dead.

I know that most Americans would be shocked at this list of national values, but I see them clearly in our behaviors and the choices we make. I also know that this is not who we want to be, so how did we get here? What happened to our ideals about life, liberty, democracy, independence, imagination?

This *devolution* of core values frequently happens to individuals, organizations, and nations. It's a gradual and nearly invisible process where values quite contrary to those we treasure seep in and grow in power as we do our work. As these contrary values are used in more and more decisions, higher principles recede into the background and have little influence. We may still think they matter, but they aren't guiding our behavior. Usually, it takes a crisis and deep distress for us to look honestly at ourselves and notice who we've become.

I feel that America is standing on the edge of an abyss, a dark night of the soul. In a dark night, meaning is lost, identity disintegrates, and we move into that most creative of spaces, chaos. W. B. Yeats powerfully describes a dark night in "The Second Coming":

> Things fall apart, the center cannot hold;
> Mere anarchy is loosed upon the world;
> The blood-dimmed tide is loosed, and everywhere
> The ceremony of innocence is drowned;
> The best lack all conviction, while the worst
> Are full of passionate intensity.

There is only one way through a dark night, and that is to illuminate the truth of who we are, surfacing the grief and regret we feel, and then reclaiming those values and principles that would bring us back to life. We need to walk willingly into the abyss, peering through the darkness to find those values, that identity, that holds its own luminosity. As we reclaim our ideals, we find the way forward, the path illuminated by our refound clarity about who we want to be.

I want to see Americans, and those who care about America, in conversation about the values and behaviors that would restore America to her intended character and original founding principles. I interpret the recent spate of books about the Founding Fathers and Mothers, the Constitutional Congress, and the American Revolution as evidence that America wants to be in this exploration. Even as I was writing this, Public Television was airing "Freedom: A History of US," while also advertising Walter Cronkite's series *Avoiding Armageddon*. How much longer will we wait to talk about these deep and troubling issues?

I've begun to invite the people I meet into conversation by asking: "What is it that you love about America? What things must be protected at all costs?" This question leads to wonderful explorations. People are energized to talk about what they love, what it means to live here as an immigrant, what they've learned about freedom, imagination, the human spirit, creativity, democracy. Even if these ideals are receding from our day-to-day experience, we realize how important it is to claim them as our own.

However, I'm also learning that it's very difficult to look truthfully at these times. It's painful to acknowledge that these ideals are no longer vibrant, that, in fact, they are dissipating. It's even more difficult to acknowledge that we must stand up and do something if we are to prevent further deterioration. It takes patience and trust in one another before we dare venture into the darkness.

I have no idea if America will acknowledge this dark night that feels so obvious to me. I can only hope some of us will be brave enough to ask, "What do I love about America that I want to preserve at all costs?" This question takes us into reflective territory, revealing the qualities of life and human community that truly inspire us. And our connection to each other strengthens as we dwell in this life-affirming space. I always leave these conversations reenergized, stronger, bolder.

At a personal level, I fear waking one morning from this awful trance that has dulled my imagination and heart, and wonder what happened to the energy and ideals I once had as an American. In his poem "The Truly Great," British poet Stephen Spender warned that we must strive "never to allow gradually the traffic to smother with noise and fog, the flowering of the spirit." Sacred values erode so slowly, lost to our awareness through subtle, darkening forces. I hope we can find the means to see through this dark night.

Beyond Hope or Fear

As the world grows ever darker, I've been forcing myself to think about hope. I watch as people far from me and near me experience more grief and suffering. Aggression and violence have moved into relationships, personal and global. Decisions are made from insecurity and fear. How is it possible to feel hopeful, to look forward to a more positive future? The biblical psalmist wrote that "without vision the people perish." Am I perishing?

I don't ask this question lightly. I am struggling to understand how I might contribute to reversing this descent into fear and sorrow, what I might do to help restore hope to the future. In the past, it was easier to believe in my own effectiveness. If I worked hard, with good colleagues and good ideas, we could make a difference. But now, I sincerely doubt that. Yet without hope that my labor will produce results, how can I keep going? If I have no belief that my visions can become real, where will I find the strength to persevere?

To answer these questions, I've consulted some who have endured dark times. They have led me on a journey into new questions, one that has taken me from hope to hopelessness, and finally, beyond hope or fear.

My journey began with a little booklet entitled *The Web of Hope* that was distributed at a global summit on development in the third world. It listed the signs of despair and hope for earth's most pressing problems. Foremost among these is the ecological destruction we humans have created. Yet the only thing the booklet lists as hopeful is that the earth works to create and maintain the conditions that support life. As the species of destruction, humans will be kicked off if we don't soon change our ways. E. O. Wilson, an eminent biologist, comments that humans are the only major species that, were we to disappear, every other species would benefit (except pets and houseplants) (Suzuki and Dressel, 1999). The Dalai Lama has been saying the same thing in many recent teachings.

This didn't make me feel hopeful.

But in the same booklet, I read a quote from Rudolf Bahro that did help: "When the forms of an old culture are dying, the new culture is created by a few people who are not afraid to be insecure." Could insecurity, self-doubt, be a good trait? I find it hard to imagine how I can work for the future without feeling grounded in the belief that my actions will make a difference. But Bahro offers a new prospect, that feeling insecure, even groundless, might actually increase my ability to stay in the work. I've read about groundlessness—especially in Buddhism—and recently have experienced it quite a bit. I haven't liked it at all, but as the dying culture turns to mush, could I give up seeking solid ground to stand on?

Vaclev Havel helped me become further attracted to insecurity and not-knowing. "Hope," he states, "is a dimension of the soul . . . an orientation of the spirit, an orientation of the heart. It transcends the world that is immediately experienced and is anchored somewhere beyond its horizons. . . . It is not the conviction that something will turn out well, but the certainty that something makes sense regardless of how it turns out."

Havel seems to be describing not hope but hopelessness, a condition beyond hope or fear when we are liberated from results, when we give up outcomes. We choose our actions because they feel right even if they will not succeed in changing things. He helps me recall the Buddhist teaching that hopelessness is not the opposite of hope. Fear is. Hope and fear are inescapable partners. Anytime we hope for a certain outcome, and work hard to make it happen, then we also introduce fear—fear of failing, fear of loss. Hopelessness is free of fear and thus can feel quite liberating. I've listened to others describe this state. Unburdened of strong emotions, they describe the miraculous appearance of clarity and energy.

Thomas Merton, the famed Christian mystic, clarified further the journey into hopelessness. In a letter to a friend, he advised:

> Do not depend on the hope of results . . . you may have to face the fact that your work will be apparently worthless and even achieve no result at all, if not perhaps results opposite to what you expect. As you get used to this idea, you start more and more to concentrate not on the results, but on the value, the rightness, the truth of the work itself. . . . You gradually struggle less and less for an idea and more and more for specific people. . . . In the end, it is the reality of personal relationship that saves everything.

I know this to be true. At Berkana, we've been working with colleagues in Zimbabwe as their country descends into violence and starvation by the actions of a madman dictator. Yet as we exchange e-mails and occasional visits, we're learning that joy is still available, not from the circumstances but from our relationships. As long as we're together, as long as we feel others supporting us, we persevere. Some of my best teachers have been younger leaders. One in her twenties said, "*How* we're going is important, not where. I want to go together and with faith." Another young Danish woman at the end of a conversation that moved us all to despair, quietly spoke: "I feel like we're holding hands as we walk into a deep, dark woods." A Zimbabwean, in her darkest moment, wrote, "In my grief I saw myself being held, us all holding one another in this incredible web of loving kindness. Grief and love in the same place. I felt as if my heart would burst with holding it all."

Thomas Merton was right. We are consoled and strengthened by being together. We don't need specific outcomes. We can live beyond hope or fear. All we need is each other.

Hopelessness has surprised me with the gift of patience. As I abandon the pursuit of effectiveness and watch my anxiety fade, patience appears. Two visionary leaders, Moses and Abraham, both carried promises given to them by their God, but they had to abandon hope that they would see these in their lifetime. They led from faith, not hope, from a relationship with something beyond their comprehension. T. S. Eliot describes this better than anyone. In "Four Quartets," he writes:

> I said to my soul, be still, and wait without hope
> for hope would be hope for the wrong thing; wait without
> love
> For love would be love of the wrong thing; there is yet faith
> But the faith and the love and the hope are all in the waiting.

This is how I want to journey through this time of increasing uncertainty. Groundless, hopeless, insecure, patient, clear. And together.

Dreaming World

I am dreaming the world. This world is an illusion. It is not as it appears.
A wise one tells me this.
"It will help you awaken," I am told.

In a moment of inattention, I scrape my index finger. It's a small cut, really nothing, but it throbs painfully. It hurts enough to keep me awake that night. This tiny break in flesh feels the full pulse of my body.

Small cuts.

I'm standing at a newsstand. *Time* magazine has a special issue, "Can the Earth Be Saved?" We humans have changed the climate and now the planet is responding to our arrogance with violent weather. Next to it is another weekly magazine featuring "Botox," the new government-approved drug that changes the face of America. It deadens facial muscles and eliminates wrinkles. To look younger, all we have to do is numb ourselves.

The world is an illusion. It is not as it appears.
Can a planet be saved by the numb at heart?

I'm driving behind a big black truck. It's been "lifted"—raised high on its chassis by big tires and supersuspension. The chrome bumper and wheels glitter with exuberance. Inside are three teenage boys, riding high, torsos dancing together to music I can't hear. I love watching them as we cruise down the road. They remind me of how it feels to own the world, those moments when it's all working just for you. Suddenly, I am weeping. The world is not as it appears.

I'm sitting on the caked and dusty surface of a reservoir that has lost its water to drought. The wind raises only dust and I feel grit from the inside out. I notice green growth on the dried surface, but when I stoop to see it, I realize it's not leaves, but algae, the first plant to appear when earth emerged from fire.

The sun sinks low and rose-colored hills appear in the east. Warmed by their radiance, I turn and face west. Cirrus clouds flame passionately, burning at sun's departure. The world is on fire. I am told, "You are watching the world dying" (who is telling me?). "In the great turnings of Life, this is the age of destruction. There is nothing to do but surrender. Gracefully. Even in death, life will be beautiful."

I am stunned by this message. I hope it is an illusion.

It is night and I am sitting on the edge of my gentle bed. I open a jar of African honey butter and begin my evening ritual. Slowly I massage cream into my pedicured feet—first the soles, then the toes, then the cuticles. From the jar's label, I learn that this cream has been gathered for me by the labor of women in Zambia and Ghana. I read that my purchase creates work for them and income for their families. I do not know how they harvest honey in Zambia or make the cream in Ghana. But I do know African women, many of them. Often I have stared at their feet with the muscular calluses from never wearing shoes, the flaking skin from never using cream.

In the peace of my bedroom, I imagine them in theirs. I know there is no comparison, not in comfort, not in security, not in fatigue. As the cream soaks into my soles, I picture them in fields, gathering the means for my life to remain soft. They cannot imagine my life. I know them well enough to know I cannot imagine theirs.

At a conference center in the United States, I am told of the African women leaders who come to meetings there. They are given their own bedrooms and never paired with a roommate. This is a gift. It's the only time they've ever had a room of their own.

I am dreaming the world. It is not as it appears. Yet I know that I spend more on a morning cup of coffee than half the world has available to live on for that entire day. Three billion people living on nothing as I walk dreamily into Starbucks.

I am dreaming the world. It is not as it appears. Yet I know that seven hundred children die every hour from starvation as I watch the cooking channel. I learn to make small cuts in the peel of a cucumber to shape it like a rose. To cut open a mango so the fruit is revealed. To slice an onion so it doesn't make me cry.

But I want to cry. For the world I am dreaming.

I turn off the television and burrow into my pillows. In Zambia just now, the women are rising from their crowded beds. Soon they will walk on hard feet into the bush, carrying basket crowns through the high grass. I hope they find where the bees hid the honey this day.

I awake and clean my coffee pot. The metal filter slices the skin under my nail, but this cut doesn't throb like the last one.

It is late afternoon in my world. The sun is still shining. The wind picks up the dust of drought and makes it difficult to see. There are still a few hours left before the sun illuminates this dust and sets the world on fire. In Africa, my sisters are sleeping now. They, too, are dreaming the world. It is not as it appears.

I leave them sleeping to go draw my bath. I have been camping and my feet are a mess. I will scrub them clean and rub away the young calluses. Then I will massage them with African honey butter. In my dreaming, I do not know where my softened soles will lead me.

A Parting Blessing

Maureen J. Hilliard, SND

May you be blessed
with vision
in these shadow times.
May light invade the darkness.
May it be a soft brilliance,
as bare as candlelight,
guiding you through
twilight 'til dawn.
And when the dawn breaks,
may you find yourself
upon a threshold.
May you enter
and go through,
and may you emerge
into the dance—
a whole and holy new
dance of grace.

Notes

Page 23   "A. R. Ammons told the same story in different and precise language": In Ammons (1976: 116).

Page 24   "In the words of the physicist Ilya Prigogine . . . " (Prigogine, 106).

Page 25   "Two biologists, Francisco Varela and Humberto Maturana, observe that life responds not to 'survival of the fittest'": Maturana, public seminar, Seattle, December 1993; see also Maturana and Varela (1992: chap. 5); Varela, Thompson, and Rosch (1991: chap. 9).

Page 31   "Brian Swimme compares our role to that of the early Christians": In *Evolution Extended*, ed. Barlow (1994: 297).

Page 34   "But theoretical biologist Stuart Kauffman has demonstrated": Kauffman (1995); Wheatley and Kellner-Rogers (1996: 31).

Page 65   "There is a clear correlation between participation and productivity": See Weisbord (1987).

Page 111 "There is a great deal of evidence for how well whole systems change processes work": See Dannemiller Tyson Associates (2000); Holman and Devane (1999); Jacobson (1994); Pratt, Gordon, and Plamping (1999); Weisbord and Janoff (1995).

Page 127 "In Christian traditions, times of chaos have been called "dark nights of the soul": See St. John of the Cross (2002).

Page 145 "A September 2000 study by a futures group from the U.S. military": See ASAF Institute (2000).

Page 147 "The Japanese approach KM differently than we do in the West": See Nonaka and Takeuchi (1995).

Page 148 "One British expert on KM": See www.skyrme.com.

Page 170 "Mohammed Junus, the founder of Grameen Bank": From a presentation at The State of the World Forum, New York City, 2001. See also Bornstein (1997).

Page 172 "Etienne Wenger, a pioneer in this field": See www.ewenger.com.

Page 177 "These communities succeed best": The Berkana Institute's processes on www.newworkspaces.net.

Page 184 "The five-stage process described here": See Trungpa (n.d.); Ray (2001).

Page 216 "Here's how Bernice Johnson Reagon": In Salzberg (1997: 151).

Page 218 "One young man who had been blinded when a policeman": In Tutu (1999: 128).

Page 219 "Archbishop Desmond Tutu describes this era": From a sermon delivered in April 1997 in North Carolina.

Page 219 "I've heard two great teachers": I heard these comments on different occasions when I was working with Somé and Palmer.

Page 261 "E. O. Wilson, an eminent biologist": In Suzuki and Dressel (1999: 13).

Page 262 "Vaclev Havel helped me become further attracted": Havel (1997).

Where These Essays Were First Published

Organizing: There Is a Simpler Way

"The New Story Is Ours to Tell": *World Business Academy/Perspectives on Business and Global Change*, June 1997

"The Promise and Paradox of Community": *The Community of the Future* (Jossey-Bass, 1998)

"Relying on Human Goodness": *Shambhala Sun*, Summer 2001

Leadership: We Make the Road by Walking

"Goodbye, Command and Control": *Leader to Leader*, July 1997

"Relying on Everyone's Creativity": *Leader to Leader*, Spring 2001

"Bringing Life to Organizational Change": *Journal for Strategic Performance Measurement*, April/May 1998

"Working with Life's Dynamics in School Systems": *Creating Successful School Systems: Voices from the University, the Field, and the Community* (Christopher-Gordon, 2001)

"When Change Is Out of Our Control": *Human Resources in the 21st Century* (Wiley, 2003)

"Leadership in Turbulent Times Is Spiritual": *Frontiers of Health Services Management*, Summer 2002

Obstacles: Where the Road Gets Hard

"The Real Work of Knowledge Management": *IHRIM Journal*, April/June 2001

"The Use and Abuses of Measurement": *Journal for Strategic Performance Measurement*, June 1999

"Name, Connect, Nourish, Illuminate: Supporting Pioneering Leaders": *Evolutionäres Management*, ed. Sonia Radatz (Verlag Systemisches Management, Austria, 2003)

"Transforming Aggression into Creativity": *Leader to Leader*, Spring 2005

Personal: Attending to Our Footsteps

"Living Our Interconnectedness": *Shambhala Sun*, Spring 2002

"Willing to Be Disturbed": *Shambhala Sun*, November 2001

"Reclaiming Time to Think": *Shambhala Sun*, September 2001

"Listening": *Shambhala Sun*, December 2001

"Raising Our Children": *Shambhala Sun*, 2002

"Ending Our Silence": *Shambhala Sun*, November 2002

My Own Footsteps

"Consumed by Either Fire or Fire": *Journal of Noetic Science*, November 1999

"Maybe You Will Be the Ones: To My Sons and Their Friends": *Imagine: What America Could Be in the 21st Century* (Rodale, June 2000)

"America's Dark Night": *Shambhala Sun*, May 2003

"Beyond Hope or Fear": *Shambhala Sun*, February 2003

"Dreaming World": *Journal of Noetic Science*, Fall 2003

Bibliography

Ammons, A. R. *Tape for the Turn of the Year.* New York: Norton, 1965.

ASAF Institute for National Security Studies and the Air University. *Beyond the Precipice—Amid Waves of Change: Strategic Scouts Explore the Future.* N.p.: Author, 2000.

Auden, W. H. *Collected Poems.* New York: Random House, 1976.

Barker, Joel. *The New Business of Paradigms* (video). www.atsmedia.com.

Barlow, Connie, ed. *Evolution Extended.* Boston: MIT Press, 1994.

Bornstein, David. *The Price of a Dream: The Story of the Grameen Bank and the Idea That Is Helping the Poor to Change Their Lives.* Chicago: University of Chicago Press, 1997.

Capra, Fritjof. *The Hidden Connections: A Science for Sustainable Living.* New York: Anchor, 2002.

———. *The Turning Point: Science, Society and the Rising Culture.* Toronto: Bantam, 1982.

———. *The Web of Life.* New York: Anchor Doubleday, 1996.

Chödrön, Pema. *The Places That Scare You: A Guide to Fearlessness in Difficult Times.* Boston: Shambhala, 2001.

———. *When Things Fall Apart.* Boston: Shambhala, 1997.

Dannemiller Tyson Associates. *Whole-Scale Change: Unleashing the Magic in Organizations.* San Francisco: Berrett-Koehler, 2000.

Eliot, T. S. *Four Quartets.* San Diego: Harcourt Brace Jovanovich, 1943.

Freire, Paulo. *Education for Critical Consciousness.* New York: Continuum, 1973.

———. *Pedagogy of the Oppressed.* New York: Herder & Herder, 1970.

Gleick, James. Chaos. *Making of a New Science.* New York: Viking, 1987.

Greenleaf, Robert K. *The Power of Servant Leadership: Essays.* San Francisco: Berrett-Koehler, 1998.

Havel, Vaclav. *The Art of the Impossible: Politics as Morality in Practice: Speeches and Writings, 1990–1996.* New York: Knopf, 1997.

Hilliard, Maureen J. *A Wrinkle on the Sole of Her Divine Feet, The Book of Blessings.* Handmade book, MJH Bookarts, 2004.

Holman, Peggy, and Tom Devane, eds. *The Change Handbook: Group Methods for Shaping the Future.* San Francisco: Berrett-Koehler, 1999.

Jacobson, Robert. *Real-time Strategic Change: How to Involve an Entire Organization in Fast and Far-reaching Change.* San Francisco: Berrett-Koehler, 1994.

Kauffman, Stuart. *At Home in the Universe: The Search for the Laws of Self-Organization and Complexity.* New York: Oxford University Press, 1995.

Kelly, Kevin. *Out of Control: The Rise of Neo-Biological Civilization.* Reading, MA: Addison-Wesley, 1994.

Kuhn, Thomas. *The Structure of Scientific Revolutions.* 3rd ed. Chicago: University of Chicago Press, 1996.

Levy, Steven. *Artificial Life.* New York: Vintage, 1992.

Margulis, Lynn. *Symbiotic Planet: A New View of Evolution.* New York: Basic Books, 1998.

Margulis, Lynn, and Dorion Sagan. *Microcosmos: Four Billion Years of Evolution from Our Microbial Ancestors.* New York: Summit, 1986.

Maturana, Humberto R., and Francisco J. Varela. *The Tree of Knowledge: The Biological Roots of Human Understanding.* Boston: Shambhala, 1992.

McDonnell, Thomas P., ed. *A Thomas Merton Reader.* Rev. ed. Garden City, NY: Image Books, 1974.

Merton, Thomas. *The Way of Chuang Tzu.* Boston: Shambhala, 1994.

Morley, Barry. *Beyond Consensus: Salvaging Sense of the Meeting.* Wallingford, PA: Pendle Hill Pamphlet 307.

Nonaka, Ikujiro, and Hirotaka Takeuchi. *The Knowledge-Creating Company: How Companies Create the Dynamics of Innovation.* New York: Oxford University Press, 1995.

Palmer, Parker J. *The Active Life: Wisdom for Work, Creativity and Caring.* San Francisco: Harper & Row, 1990.

Pasternak, Boris. *The Poetry of Boris Pasternak, 1917–1959.* Boston: Putnam, 1959.

Pratt, Julian, Pat Gordon, and Diane Plamping. *Working Whole Systems: Putting Theory into Practice in Organizations.* London: King's Fund, 1999.

Prigogine, Ilya. "Exploring Complexity." *European Journal of Operational Research* 30 (1987): 97–103.

Ray, Reginald. *Secrets of the Vajra World.* Boston: Shambhala, 2001.

Remen, Rachel Naomi. *My Grandfather's Blessings: Stories of Strength, Refuge, and Belonging.* New York: Riverhead, 2000.

Salzberg, Sharon. *A Heart as Wide as the World.* Boston: Shambhala, 1997.

Somé, Malidoma. *The Healing Wisdom of Africa.* New York: Tarcher, 1998.

Spender, Stephen. *Collected Poems.* New York: Random House, 1955.

St. John of the Cross. *Dark Night of the Soul.* Trans. and introduction by Mirabai Starr. New York: Riverhead, 2002.

Suzuki, David, and Holly Dressel. *From Naked Ape to Superspecies.* Toronto: Stoddart, 1999.

Swimme, Brian, and Thomas Berry. *The Universe Story: From the Primordial Flaring Forth to the Exozoic Era—A Celebration of the Unfolding of the Cosmos.* San Francisco: HarperSanFrancisco, 1991.

Trungpa, Chögyam. *Secret beyond Thought.* Boston: Shambhala, n.d.

Tutu, Desmond Mpilo. *No Future without Forgiveness.* London: Rider, 1999.

Varela, Francisco, Evan Thompson, and Eleanor Rosch. *The Embodied Mind: Cognitive Science and Human Experience.* Cambridge, MA: MIT Press, 1991.

Walton, Mary. *The Deming Management Method.* New York: Penguin Putnam, 1986.

Weisbord, Marvin. *Productive Workplaces Revisited: Dignity, Meaning, and Community in the 21st Century.* San Francisco: Jossey-Bass, 2003.

Whyte, David. *Crossing the Unknown Sea.* New York: Riverhead, 2001.

———. *The Heart Aroused.* New York: Currency Doubleday, 1994.

Weisbord, Marvin, and Sandra Janoff. *Future Search: An Action Guide to Finding Common Ground in Organizations and Communities.* San Francisco: Berrett-Koehler, 1995.

Wenger, Etienne, Richard McDermott, and William Snyder. *Cultivating Communities of Practice.* Cambridge, MA: Harvard Business School Press, 2002.

Wheatley, Margaret J., and Myron Kellner-Rogers. *A Simpler Way.* San Francisco: Berrett-Koehler, 1996.

Yeats, W. B. *The Collected Poems of W. B. Yeats.* Ed. Richard J. Finneran. New York: Collier, 1983.

Permissions and Photo Credits

Maureen J. Hilliard, SND, "A Parting Blessing" used with permission of author.

T.S. Eliot from *Four Quartets*, used with permission of Harcourt Brace.

Two opening photos: Cloud with silver lining, School of fish, used with permission of © Getty Images

Closing photograph: Cham women returning from market, Indochina 1952 (Vietnam/Cambodia) © Werner Bischof, used with permission of Magnum Photos.

All other photographs: © 2004 Margaret J. Wheatley

Index

failure rate in corporations, 101
feedback and measurements in, 158, 159, 160
learning in, 85, 97, 111
in living systems, 75–76, 85–86, 94, 105–106
local and individual initiatives in, 68, 70–71, 178
as long-term effort, 71–72
in meaning, 104–105
mechanistic approach to, 84–85
participation in, 79–80, 88–90
personal, affecting leaders, 72–73
principles of, 88–96
   compared to models, 95–96
   compared to techniques, 93–95
questions on critical issues in, 97–98
resistance to, 28, 83
in self-organizing systems, 33, 68
in uncertain and turbulent times, 104–105, 114–133
Chaos
   in cycles of life, 127–128
   knowledge creation and management in, 145, 153
   and order in complex systems, 34–36, 39
   in uncertain and turbulent times, 114–133
      importance of organizational identity in, 118–119
      spiritual leadership in, 125–133
   and willingness to be disturbed, 210–213
Chemical plant safety performance, 42–43, 51, 52
Chief Seattle, 204
Children
   demanding schedules and stress of, 222–225
   distribution of car safety seats for, 78
   on Lake Powell boat trip, 245–256
      creativity of, 249, 253, 254
      critical strengths of, 251–254
      diversity of, 248–249, 252, 254
      hopes of, 247–248
      relationships of, 249, 250, 252–253
      views on future, 247
   listening to, 220
   in school systems. See School systems

Chitwood, Michael, 91
Chödrön, Pema, 14
Choices
   on compliance with directives, 86–87, 90–91, 149
   on noticing or responding to new information, 37, 46, 85, 169–170, 236–237
   on participation in change, 105–106
   on speaking out in disturbing information, 226–229
CIDA City Campus in South Africa, 165–166
Civil rights movement, 216–217
Coherence in self-organizing systems, 68–70
Command and control leadership, 64–67, 126, 183
Commitment
   in communities of practice, 177
   in enduring organizations, 73–74
   and identity in self-organizing systems, 38
   and participation in self-organizing systems, 67–68, 70
   in problem solving, 195, 196
Communication
   compared to finding shared significance, 88
   of meaningful information, network capacity for, 109–110
   questions in assessment of, 97, 98
   and speaking out on disturbing information, 226–229, 259–260
   in uncertain times, 119–121
      honest and quick flow of information in, 120–121
      in organization sponsored informal gatherings, 119–120
   with youth during Lake Powell boat trip, 245–256
Community
   boundaries and relationships in, 48, 52
   diversity in, 48–49, 50, 51
   identity and clarity of shared purpose in, 50–52, 54
   instinct of, 45, 47
   leaders in, 170–178
      essential activities supporting, 173–175
   learning in, 170–173

in South Africa, leadership development in, 165–166

Science
limitations of, 125
in old and new stories of life, 18, 22, 23
premises of, 16

Self-creation, 24–25, 27
in definition of life, 46
freedom in, and change, 86–88

Self-determination need, compared to need for relationships, 46–54

Self-organization, 33–44
in communities of practice, 34, 172
in complex systems, 93–94
contributions and innovations in, 29
in disaster and crisis situations, 33, 118, 124
dynamics of, 41–43
identity in, 37–39, 66
and coherence, 68–70
individual initiatives in, 68, 70–71
information in, 39–40, 41–43
and localized change activity, 68
knowledge management in, 152
leadership in, 43–44, 66
long-term approach to change efforts in, 71–72
as naturally occurring process, 25–27
problem solving in, 29, 42–43, 68
productivity in, 65
relationships in, 40–41
trust in, 44, 112–113

Servant leadership, 30, 126

Service to others
happiness and joy in, 128–129
in meaningful work, 121–122, 128
in servant leadership, 30, 126
of students in South Africa, 165–166

"Seven Hundred Years to Go," 198–199

Silence, compared to speaking out on issues, 226–229

Simulations in planning process, 121

Skyrme, David, 148

Somé, Malidoma, 45, 219–220, 273n

South Africa
apartheid system in, 218–219, 228
student leaders from CIDA City Campus in, 165–166

Spender, Stephen, 260

Spiritual issues
in hopelessness, 261, 262–263, 264
in interconnectedness, 129, 204
and listening, 219, 220
in leadership, 125–133
personal measures of, 129, 132
in old story of life, 19
in poetry of Eliot, 236–244
in poverty, 1

Stereotypes and labeling of behavior, 81–82, 109

Strategic planning, uncertainty affecting, 116–117

Stress
behavior changes in, 115–116
and demanding schedules of children, 222–225
information flow and communication in, 120–121
in organization sponsored informal gatherings, 119–120
in organizational aggression, 183
personal contacts and relationships in, 122–123
rituals and symbols used in, 122

Surprise, acceptance and expectation of, 81–82, 132, 241
in feedback, 159
in willingness to be disturbed, 212

"Surrender," 137–138

Survival of the fit and fittest, 25, 47

Swimme, Brian, 17, 31, 272n

Symbols and rituals
bonfire of beliefs in, 240
in uncertain times, 122

T

Teamwork
measurements of, 157, 160
in problem solving, 195, 196

Technology
environmental impact of, 245
facilitating community connections, 174
in knowledge management, 147, 152–153
in old story of life, 18
in school system, 108–109

Termites, complex and coordinated behavior
of, 35–36
Terrorist activities
anthrax incidents in, 205–206
on September 11, 2002, 115, 117, 118,
119, 124, 128
Thera Island, ancient culture in, 6–8
Thinking, taking time for, 130–131, 208,
214–217
in knowledge creation and management,
153–154
in meetings, 130–131
for personal spiritual health, 131
"The True Professional" (Palmer), 134
Trust, 70
in self-organizing organizations, 44,
112–113
Tutu, Desmond, 219, 273n
Tzu, Chuang, 62

U
Uncertainty, 113–133
behavior changes in, 115–116
boundaries as protection in, 205–206
from disturbing information, 104–105,
210–213
hopelessness in, 262–264
information flow and communication in,
104–105, 120–121
leadership in, 116, 125–133
meaning as motivation in, 121–122
organizational identity in, 118–119
relationships and connections in, 117–118,
119–120, 124
difficulties in, 123
in direct personal contacts, 122–123
importance of, 263
in organization sponsored informal
gatherings, 119–120
rituals and symbols used in, 122

simulations in preparation for, 121
strategic planning in, 116–117
United Airlines, 119
Unity
in problem solving, 190
in shared meaning and diversity, 80–81

V
Values
in dark time for United States, 257–260
and hopelessness, 261–264
in organizational identity, 118–119
and poetry of Eliot, 236–244
of youth, 247–256
Varela, Francisco, 25, 37, 46, 92, 272n

W
The Web of Hope, 261
Webs of relationships, 106–107, 204, 237
interconnectedness in, 204–209
resiliency in, 106–107, 204
in spiritual leadership, 129
unintended consequences of actions in,
207–208
Weisbord, Marvin, 65
Welch, Jack, 72
Wenger, Etienne, 172, 272n
Whitman, Walt, 234
Wilson, E. O., 261, 273n
Work-to-rule actions, 29
World Wide Web, 246
access to information in, 144
relationships and community in, 49–50
self-organization in, 34

Y
Yeats, W. B., 258

Z
Zimbabwe, 263

About the Author

Margaret (Meg) Wheatley writes, teaches, and speaks about radically new practices and ideas for organizing in chaotic times. She has worked in virtually every type of organization and all continents (excluding Antarctica). The consistent focus of her work has been to encourage people to organize as life does—cooperatively, generously, systemically, and nonhierarchically. She seeks to create organizations where people are seen as the blessing, not the problem.

Meg is president of The Berkana Institute, a charitable global foundation serving and linking life-affirming leaders in many countries. She was an organizational consultant for thirty years, as well as a professor of management in two graduate programs. She began work as a public school teacher and urban education administrator in New York City and as a Peace Corps volunteer teaching in Korea.

Meg's work appears in three award-winning books—*Leadership and the New Science* (1992, 1999), *A Simpler Way* (coauthored with Myron Rogers, 1996), and *Turning to One Another: Simple Conversations to Restore Hope to the Future* (2002)—plus several videos and articles. Meg draws many of her ideas from new science; increasingly, her ideas about leadership and organizations are gleaned from her understanding of many different cultures and spiritual traditions.

The Berkana Institute is a global charitable foundation dedicated to serving life-affirming leaders. Since 1992, Berkana has experimented with the new ideas, processes, and structures that represent the future of organizing, and has worked with people of all ages in more than forty countries. Using multiple means, Berkana supports local leaders who are working to create communities and organizations that rely on the creativity, caring, and commitment of everyone. Berkana has discovered that the world is blessed with tens of thousands of these leaders—they are young and old, in all countries, working in education, non-profits, community development, governments, businesses. They are courageous people discovering successful ways to create positive change in their local communities, villages, and organizations. Berkana supports them by providing resources, ideas, and methods for use in their local communities. Berkana also connects these leaders to one another, aspiring to create a global community of life-affirming leaders. See www.berkana.org.

Meg received her doctorate from Harvard University's program in Administration, Planning, and Social Policy. She holds an M.A. in communications and systems thinking from New York University and a B.A. in history and English from the University of Rochester, New York, and University College London, England. She has received numerous awards and honorary doctorates. The American Society for Training and Development has honored her with the title "a living legend."

Meg lives in the mountains of Utah, where she occasionally rests after long journeys, and takes time to be with her adult children, grandchildren, horses, and friends.

Her articles and work appear at www.margaretwheatley.com.

Revolutionary Acts for Finding Our Way
A DVD Series

Join Margaret Wheatley, via DVD, in a personal exploration of some of the critical issues raised in Finding Our Way. *Each DVD focuses on what Meg terms 'revolutionary acts'. In her intimate, conversational style, Meg encourages you to ask certain questions, to notice your own behaviors, and to commit to creating real change through simple, consistent, and conscious actions.*

As Meg explains: 'If we are to bring about significant changes in how we organize, then there are several actions we each need to take. Each of these is startlingly simple, yet profoundly effective. But nothing much will change for the better unless we each step forward as courageous champions of these simple acts.'

The first three DVDs in this series are:

1. **Finding Our Way: It's About Time.** In this DVD, Meg focuses on the necessity for taking time to think, learning from our experience, and reflecting with colleagues, behaviors which are quickly disappearing in most organizations. She offers piercing questions and tried and true practices for reintroducing thinking into our lives.

2. **Finding Our Way: From Hero to Host.** Here you are encouraged to think past the images of heroic leadership to a new role as leader, one who hosts the processes that bring people together to do their work. This style of leadership is required if we are to evoke the intelligence, creativity and caring of people throughout our organizations and communities.

3. **Finding Our Way: Depending on Diversity.** This is an exploration into a new way of looking at diversity--not as a problem, but as a life-saving, survival capacity for organizations and communities. Only by seeking out differences do we develop a clear understanding of what is going on, and how we might truly address the complex issues facing us. Meg describes practices for weaving together the multitude of perspectives that we each have, and for finding common ground.

Berrett-Koehler Publishers

Berrett-Koehler is an independent publisher of books and other publications at the leading edge of new thinking and innovative practice on work, business, management, leadership, stewardship, career development, human resources, entrepreneurship, and global sustainability.

Since the company's founding in 1992, we have been committed to creating a world that works for all by publishing books that help us to integrate our values with our work and work lives, and to create more humane and effective organizations.

We have chosen to focus on the areas of work, business, and organizations, because these are central elements in many people's lives today. Furthermore, the work world is going through tumultuous changes, from the decline of job security to the rise of new structures for organizing people and work. We believe that change is needed at all levels—individual, organizational, community, and global—and our publications address each of these levels.

To find out about our new books, special offers, free excerpts, and much more, subscribe to our free monthly eNewsletter at **www.bkconnection.com**.

More books from Margaret J. Wheatley

Turning to One Another
Simple Conversations to Restore Hope to the Future
By Margaret J. Wheatley

Margaret Wheatley argues eloquently that the innovative ideas so badly needed to resolve social problems and restore optimism and hope will never come from governments, corporations, or "official" organizations, but from the ageless process of people thinking together in conversation.

2002, paperback original, 144 pages • ISBN 1-57675-145-7 Item #5147-530 • $16.95

Leadership and the New Science
Discovering Order in a Chaotic World
Second Edition, Completely Revised and Expanded
By Margaret J. Wheatley

In this revised edition of the international bestseller, Wheatley shows how the "New Science"—revolutionary discoveries in quantum physics, chaos theory, and biology that are overturning centuries-old images of the universe—provides powerful insights into the design, leadershop, and management of organizations.

2001, paperback, 215 pages • ISBN 1-57675-119-8 Item #51198-530 • $19.95

A Simpler Way
By Margaret J. Wheatley and Myron Kellner-Rogers

This poetic book explores the primary question: How could we organize human endeavor if we developed different understandings of how life organizes itself?

1999, paperback, 168 pages • ISBN 1-57675-050-7 Item #50507-530 • $19.95

Berrett-Koehler Publishers
PO Box 565, Williston, VT 05495-9900
Call toll-free! 800-929-2929 7am-9pm Eastern Standard Time
Or fax your order to 802-864-7626
For fastest service order online: **www.bkconnection.com**

Spread the Word!

Berrett-Koehler books are available at quantity discounts for orders of 10 or more copies. To find out about discounts for orders of 10 or more copies for individuals, corporations, institutions, and organizations, please call us toll-free at (800) 929-2929.

Finding Our Way
Leadership for an Uncertain Time
By Margaret J. Wheatley

2005, hardcover, 304 pages • ISBN 978-1-57675-317-0 Item #53170 • $27.95

To find out about our discount programs for resellers, please contact our Special Sales department at (415) 288-0260; Fax: (415)362-2512; or email us at **bkpub@bkpub.com**.

Subscribe to our free eNewsletter!

To find out what's happening at Berrett-Koehler and to receive announcements of our new books, special offers, free excerpts, and much more, subscibe to our free monthly eNewsletter at **www.bkconnection.com**.

Berrett-Koehler Publishers
PO Box 565, Williston, VT 05495-9900
Call toll-free! 800-929-2929 7am-9pm Eastern Standard Time
Or fax your order to 802-864-7626
For fastest service order online: **www.bkconnection.com**